"This monograph is an absolute first in the field of Persian studies and as such must be considered seminal, not only in its approach to literature, but also because it has managed to meticulously bring to purview pragmatics, discourse analysis, and other cognitive sciences as pertains to literature at large under the rubric of one of the greatest poets of not only the Persian-speaking world but also the world over—Sa'dī. It is dynamic in its approach and unapologetic in inspiring daring approaches to literary works. Every chapter of this monograph will engage the reader so to ponder their otherwise "well-established" notions of comprehension of the written word—and understanding of hermeneutics. Kudos to the authors!"

Alireza Korangy, Editor-in-Chief, *International Journal of Persian Literature*

Evidentiality in Sa'dī's Poetry and Prose

This study is the first to introduce evidentiality to the stylistic analysis of literary works, specifically that of the great Persian writer Sa'dī, focusing on how he used linguistic means to illustrate a real or ideational world.

The authors begin by introducing the concept of evidentiality; its definition, its coding in Persian, the rationale behind evidentiality analysis, and semantic-pragmatic functions of evidentiality. The book highlights how evidentiality can be accounted for as a stylistic device to reveal the validity of a narration, as well as the author's commitment and contribution to it. Three of Sa'dī's major works are analyzed—*Būstān*, *Golestān*, and *Sonnets*—using Krippendoff's frequency approach. It is argued that Sa'dī deployed an array of evidentials in his work, from direct visual evidentials in *Golestān* and *Sonnets* to heard and quoted evidentials in *Būstān*. To illustrate this, the book includes translations of Sa'dī's poetry and prose. In addition, the authors consider historical and contemporary manifestations of the Persian narrative style, as well as exploring the cultural concerns of the Persian speech community.

The book will appeal to general linguists, practitioners of pragmatics and stylistics, literary critics, and those interested in contrastive analysis of literature and cultural studies.

Behrooz Mahmoodi-Bakhtiari is Associate Professor of Linguistics and Persian at the Faculty of Fine Arts, University of Tehran, as well as being an affiliate at the Institute of Oriental Studies, Russian-Armenian University, Yerevan. He received his PhD in linguistics from Allameh Tabatabaee University in 2004. His major fields of work are Persian linguistics and Iranian dialectology, as well as discourse analysis of drama and fiction. He is the author of the books *Tense in Persian* (2002), *Fārsi Biyāmuzim/ Let's Learn Persian* (2003), *Persian for Dummies* (2015), *Pande Pārsi/Listening Comprehension of Persian* (2016), and *Salām Doktor/Dialogue Activities of Persian*.

Masoumeh Mehrabi is Assistant Professor of Linguistics at Ayatollah Boroujerdi University, in Boroujerd, Iran. Her main research interests include sociolinguistics, psycholinguistics, stylistics, and discourse analysis. Her major publication in English about the Persian language is "Lexical Information of Persian Transitive Verbs during Listening Comprehension."

Iranian Studies
Series editors: Homa Katouzian
University of Oxford

Mohamad Tavakoli-Targhi
University of Toronto

Since 1967 the International Society for Iranian Studies (ISIS) has been a leading learned society for the advancement of new approaches in the study of Iranian society, history, culture, and literature. The new ISIS Iranian Studies series published by Routledge will provide a venue for the publication of original and innovative scholarly works in all areas of Iranian and Persianate Studies.

43 **Foreign Policy of the Islamic Republic of Iran**
   Between Ideology and Pragmatism
   Przemyslaw Osiewicz

44 **Secularization of Islam in Post-Revolutionary Iran**
   Mahmoud Pargoo

45 **Iran's Green Movement**
   Everyday Resistance, Political Contestation and Social Mobilization
   Navid Pourmokhtari

46 **Poetry and Revolution**
   The Poets and Poetry of the Constitutional Era of Iran
   Edited by Homa Katouzian and Alireza Korangy

47 **Translating Rumi into the West**
   A Linguistic Conundrum and Beyond
   Amir Sedaghat

48 **Evidentiality in Sa'dī's Poetry and Prose**
   A Corpus Stylistic Study
   Behrooz Mahmoodi-Bakhtiari and Masoumeh Mehrabi

For more information about this series, please visit: www.routledge.com/middleeaststudies/series/IRST

Evidentiality in Sa'dī's Poetry and Prose
A Corpus Stylistic Study

Behrooz Mahmoodi-Bakhtiari and Masoumeh Mehrabi

LONDON AND NEW YORK

First published 2023
by Routledge
4 Park Square, Milton Park, Abingdon, Oxon OX14 4RN

and by Routledge
605 Third Avenue, New York, NY 10158

Routledge is an imprint of the Taylor & Francis Group, an informa business

© 2023 Behrooz Mahmoodi-Bakhtiari and Masoumeh Mehrabi

The right of Behrooz Mahmoodi-Bakhtiari and Masoumeh Mehrabi to be identified as authors of this work has been asserted in accordance with sections 77 and 78 of the Copyright, Designs and Patents Act 1988.

All rights reserved. No part of this book may be reprinted or reproduced or utilised in any form or by any electronic, mechanical, or other means, now known or hereafter invented, including photocopying and recording, or in any information storage or retrieval system, without permission in writing from the publishers.

Trademark notice: Product or corporate names may be trademarks or registered trademarks, and are used only for identification and explanation without intent to infringe.

British Library Cataloguing-in-Publication Data
A catalogue record for this book is available from the British Library

Library of Congress Cataloging-in-Publication Data
Names: Maḥmūdī Bakhtiyārī, Bihrūz, 1973 or 1974– author. | Mehrabi, Masoumeh, author.
Title: Evidentiality in Saʻdī's poetry and prose : a corpus stylistic study / Behrooz Mahmoodi-Bakhtiari, Masoumeh Mehrabi.
Description: Abingdon, Oxon ; New York, NY : Routledge, 2023. | Series: Iranian studies | Includes bibliographical references and index.
Identifiers: LCCN 2022049499 (print) | LCCN 2022049500 (ebook) | ISBN 9781032443607 (hardback) | ISBN 9781032443621 (paperback) | ISBN 9781003371786 (ebook)
Subjects: LCSH: Saʻdī—Criticism and interpretation. | Saʻdī—Language. | Evidentials (Linguistics)
Classification: LCC PK6546 .M255 2023 (print) | LCC PK6546 (ebook) | DDC 891/.5511—dc23/eng/20221102
LC record available at https://lccn.loc.gov/2022049499
LC ebook record available at https://lccn.loc.gov/2022049500

ISBN: 978-1-032-44360-7 (hbk)
ISBN: 978-1-032-44362-1 (pbk)
ISBN: 978-1-003-37178-6 (ebk)

DOI: 10.4324/9781003371786

Typeset in Times New Roman
by Apex CoVantage, LLC

Contents

List of tables ix
Preface x
Acknowledgements xii
Abbreviations; note on transliteration conventions of
Persian transcripts xiii

Introduction 1

1 Evidentiality 4

1.1 Evidentiality in language 4
    1.1.1 Evidentiality in languages of the world 8
1.2 Evidentiality in literature 15

2 Theoretical considerations 18

2.1 Evidentiality as a pragmatic device 18
    2.1.1 Reported speech 18
2.2 Evidentiality as a stylistic device 25
    2.2.1 The definition of style 25

3 Evidentiality in Sa'dī's masterpieces 29

3.1 Būstān (Sa'dī, 1396a) 29
3.2 Golestān (Sa'dī, 1396b) translated
    by F. Gladwin (1865) 83
3.3 Sonnets (Sa'dī, 2002/1382) 136

4 Evidentiality in the three literary works 159

4.1 Cross-comparison of evidentials in the three
    masterpieces 159

4.2 Peculiarities of Sa'dī's literary style in Būstān, Golestān, and Sonnets 159
4.3 The function of direct reported speech 161

5 Conclusions 163

5.1 Modern stylistics 163
5.2 Literary and cognitive implications of evidentiality 164
5.3 A snapshot of the book 166

Glossary of terms 168
Index 169

Tables

3.1	Frequency of evidentials in the first chapter of *Būstān*	30
3.2	Frequency of evidentials in second chapter of *Būstān*	41
3.3	Frequency of evidentials in third chapter of *Būstān*	48
3.4	Frequency of evidentials in fourth chapter of *Būstān*	54
3.5	Frequency of evidentials in fifth chapter of *Būstān*	59
3.6	Frequency of evidentials in sixth chapter of *Būstān*	63
3.7	Frequency of evidentials in seventh chapter of *Būstān*	66
3.8	Frequency of evidentials in eighth chapter of *Būstān*	73
3.9	Frequency of evidentials in ninth chapter of *Būstān*	76
3.10	Frequency of evidentials in tenth chapter of *Būstān*	80
3.11	The overall results of evidentiality frequency in *Būstān*	82
3.12	Frequency of evidentials in *Būstān*	82
3.13	Frequency of evidentials in first chapter of *Golestān*	84
3.14	Frequency of evidentials in second chapter of *Golestān*	92
3.15	Frequency of evidentials in third chapter of *Golestān*	104
3.16	Frequency of evidentials in fourth chapter of *Golestān*	112
3.17	Frequency of evidentials in fifth chapter of *Golestān*	116
3.18	Frequency of evidentials in sixth chapter of *Golestān*	121
3.19	Frequency of evidentials in seventh chapter of *Golestān*	124
3.20	Frequency of evidentials in eighth chapter of *Golestān*	129
3.21	The overall results of evidentiality frequency in *Golestān*	134
3.22	Frequency of evidentials in *Golestān*	135
3.23	Frequency of evidentials in *Sonnets*	158
4.1	Cross-comparison of evidentials in the masterpieces	160

Preface

It does matter *how* we say things, at least as far as the formulation of literary texts is concerned. This book considers the potential of pragmatic and cognitive theory as a tool for the stylistic analysis of *evidentiality* in literary texts. Evidentiality, known as the linguistic encoding of source of information, is of pivotal concern to many researchers working both within the framework of theoretical linguistics (like syntacticians, morphologists, semanticists, and experts in pragmatics or discourse analysis) and those specialized in fields beyond the scope of linguistics (like journalists, experts of critical discourse analysis, and even political analysts).

Evidentiality, when considered in literary works, can be the common ground of some fields of studies, namely stylistics, narratology, and literary criticism (both cognitive and formal or structural). Here, the general purpose is to demonstrate the issues and illustrate the explanation for application of evidentiality as used in literary works to achieve an important function, which is to depict the realistic or ideational viewpoint by the use of language and linguistic markers. The application and employment of direct visual evidentials is much more than the heard one in *Golestān*, representing that Sa'dī has seen and experienced the theme of the stories much more directly than what has been explained in *Būstān*. It shows how language mirrors thought. The findings will be compared with the results of the analysis of evidentiality as represented in Sa'dī's *Sonnets*, in which, based on the generic characteristics of love poetry, there will be found more sonnets without evidential markers and less with evidentials (mostly direct seen/visual type).

This is a monograph that can be utilized by general linguists, practitioners of pragmatics and stylistics, literary critics, and those interested in contrastive analysis of literature and cultural studies. As translation of numerous proses and poems will be provided, it can serve as a secondary source of information for any interested student of Persian language and literature. It can also be useful for cultural linguists, for this analysis will shed light on some cultural aspects of old Persian narrative style, and it can pave the way for comparison of old and new narrative style in Persian. It can also show some remarkable points about the cultural considerations and concerns of the Persian speech community, especially when reported speech and its functions in the given speech community is discussed.

Acknowledgements

We would like to thank the well-known publisher Routledge for the encouragement, support, and much appreciated advice throughout the development of the ideas and research covered in this monograph.

We as the authors make a plea for further considerations from the readers' attention, for this work is far from being the last words on evidentiality in Persian literary works. We sincerely welcome suggestions, counterexamples, and refinements in order to improve the book.

Abbreviations; note on transliteration conventions of Persian transcripts

Persian transliteration symbol	Closest IPA sound symbol	Closest sound and example (from English)
u	/u:/	"oo" as in *pool*
ā	/a:/	"a" as in *father*
a	/æ/	"a" as in *cat*
e (including word final)	/ɛ/	"e" as in *set*
x	/x/	Voiceless velar fricative
q	/q/	Voiceless uvular stop
'/'	/'/	Glottal stop as in Sa'dī
sh	/ʃ/	"sh" as in *shy*
zh	/ʒ/	"s" as in *pleasure*
ch	/tʃ/	"ch" as in *church*
j	/ĵ/	"dʒ" as in jump

Introduction

This monograph addresses evidentiality in literary masterpieces; evidentiality, defined as the grammatical encoding of the information source, is of interest to theoretical linguists, cognitive scientists, typologists, anthropologists, and even journalists in recent years. Evidentiality is a kind of indexicality in which the evidential form indexes the relation between the speaker, the object or event spoken about, and the linguistic act of producing evidential utterance. As a linguistic strategy, it can be used to specify some of the stylistic peculiarities of great works of literature like Sa'dī's masterpieces. The rationale behind this perspective is that in every language one can find means for saying how one knows what one is talking about. These are means of phrasing inferences, assumptions, probabilities, possibilities, quotations in a variety of ways. These kinds of wording show whether the speaker saw the event happen, didn't see it but heard it, or made a general assumption or inference. As, for the first time, Franz Boas (1938: 133) put it, "some languages consider source of information as an obligatory aspect whether seen, heard, or inferred and encode them grammatically."

In Persian, this aspect of information source encoding is manifested lexically, not grammatically. Verbs of seeing, hearing, assuming, reporting, and some semantic aspects of perfect aspect index evidentiality. The present study investigates evidentiality as a stylistic means contributing to the achievement of the author's aim. This monograph highlights the intentional application and employment of evidentials on the author's part as a discourse marker that shows the validity of the author's intended theme manifested in the narration.

This study focuses on semantic-pragmatic functions of evidentiality in three of Sa'dī's masterpieces, namely *Būstān*, *Golestān*, and *Sonnets*. The main question here is how Sa'dī, as the writer or poet, has used linguistic means to illustrate a real/ideational world in *Būstān* and *Golestān*, respectively, and a love realm in *Sonnets*. Content analysis (Krippendoff's frequency approach) has been used as the method of analysis—as a

DOI: 10.4324/9781003371786-1

quantitative methodology in corpus stylistic studies. As for the results, they show that in *Būstān*, *Golestān*, and *Sonnets* there can be found narratives and stories in which the author prefers not to use any evidential, but the prominent tendency in *Būstān* is using heard and quoted evidentials, and in *Golestān* and *Sonnets* directly seen and observed evidentials. It seems that Sa'dī has applied linguistic evidentiality consciously to illustrate the realm of an ideational truth in *Būstān* and the realm of experienced and observed reality in *Golestān*. Again, in *Sonnets*, because of the generic characteristics of love poems (the urgent need for the description of the beloved beauty and features) the direct seen/visual evidentials have been used more often.

Here, the general purpose is to illustrate the explanation for application of evidentiality as used in literary works to achieve an important function, which is to depict the realistic or ideational viewpoint or love life by the use of language and linguistic markers. Of course, it is an "*illustration*," for data supports the views discussed here. The application and employment of direct visual evidentials is much more than the heard one in *Golestān*, representing that Sa'dī has seen and experienced the theme of the stories much more directly than what is explained in *Būstān*. It shows how language mirrors thought.

In the first chapter, the outstanding question will be: What are the evidentials good for from a pure linguistic aspect? First, they are the indications of the speaker's degree of commitment to the information mentioned, so that the speaker qualifies the validity of the proposition. Second, evidentiality is used to clarify a concrete perspective by specifying the details of the statement and vividness of a fact or story. Third, they are used as a form of social action to show the avoidance of being wrong, to be precise, to show the speaker's ability to remember the details of the information source. This is called epistemological stance—a stand speakers take on how they acquired the information, how they know it (Mushin, 2001). Fourth, they show the speaker's stance and position within the community. Aikhenvald (2018) mentioned Mamaindê as a language in which evidentiality use equals to a mechanism of face saving. In this language, the avoidance of being wrong in narration is related to the avoidance of losing face. There, evidentials provide the speaker with a way of saving face in speech in a community in which one's words represent one's character. So, the employment of such a linguistic strategy can have some cultural connotations.

The primary question in the second chapter is what are the evidentials good for in literature, from a literary theory point of view? Ifantidou (2001) believes that evidentials have two main functions: to indicate the source of knowledge and to indicate the speaker's degree of certainty about the proposition. In this chapter, the semantic-pragmatic function of this linguistic strategy in encountered, as well as a stylistic device serving literature.

The sociocultural aspects of reported speech in Persian is discussed in the second chapter, for, as will be seen, there are plenty of instances in which Sa'dī has used reported speech. Certainly in literature, it shows the validity attributed to the stories from the author's part.

The third chapter deals with the evidentiality manifested in the given masterpieces. This will be a detailed analysis.

The fourth chapter compares the arrangement and application of this linguistic marker as is used in *Būstān*, *Golestān*, and *Sonnets*. The (historical, logical, and even cultural) reasons behind Sa'dī's preferences leading to such peculiarities are explained in this chapter.

The last chapter deals with the concluding remarks as derived from the concise analysis of the related instances of the masterpieces, some of which are discussed herein. In the last chapter, some cognitive, stylistic, and functional explanations are presented, beside a snapshot of the book.

This is a monograph that can be utilized by (cultural) linguists, practitioners of pragmatics and stylistics, literary critics, those interested in contrastive analysis of literature, and cognitive linguists. As translation of numerous examples of prose and poems are provided, it can serve as a secondary source of information for any interested student of Persian language and literature. It can also be useful for cultural linguists, for this analysis sheds light on some cultural aspects of old Persian narrative style, and it can pave the way for comparison of old and new narrative style in Persian.

Reference list

Aikhenvald, A. (2018). Evidentiality: The Framework. In Aikhenvald, A (ed.). *Oxford Handbook of Evidentiality*. Oxford: Oxford University Press.
Boas, F. (1938). Language. In F. Boas (ed.), *General Anthropology*. Boston: O.C. Health and Company. (pp. 124–145).
Ifantidou, E. (2001). *Evidentials and Relavance*. Amsterdam: John Benjamins Publishing Company.
Mushin, I. (2001). *Evidentiality and Epistemological Stance; Narrative Retelling*. Amsterdam: John Benjamins Publishing Company.

1 Evidentiality

Introduction

Humans use various cognitive or natural (direct) experiences to figure out new information about the world around them. For human beings, information about the world can be gained directly through various perceptual processes (e.g. *seeing* an accident happened) or indirectly through communication or various types of inferences (e.g. *figuring out* that the accident has happened based on the clues or signs). These experiences (e.g. visual or auditory perception, hearsay, quoted information, inference, and argumentations) that characterize the conditions under which we discover information are known as *sources of information* (Johnson, Hashtroudi and Lindsay, 1993 as mentioned in Unal, 2018). The process of attributing a piece of information to a specific source is known as *source monitoring* (Johnson, 1988 as mentioned in Unal, 2018). Meanwhile, human languages have some devices to encode sources of information. This process of attributing some source of information to the statements manifests itself in language. Linguists call this manifestation "evidentiality," and they call the linguistic devices "evidentials."

Moreover, some other pragmatic functions can be attributed to evidentiality: the speaker's commitment to the information contained in the expressed sentence, reliability of the information, precision on the part of the reporter or information conveyed, probability, and the expectation concerning that probability of the information expressed. Meanwhile, evidentiality is related to the cognitive concept of "trust" (Morady Moghaddam, 2019). All of these relations are covered in detail in the discussion of reported speech.

1.1 Evidentiality in language

By evidentiality one marks the source of information contained in a statement, and as the speaker he/she indicates how one has gained or learned that piece of information. Languages differ in how to mark an information source linguistically.

DOI: 10.4324/9781003371786-2

According to Murray (2017: 9), the semantic behavior of evidentials, and other markers that encode evidentiality, has been studied for a wide variety of languages, including Turkish (Izvorski, 1997), Bulgarian (Izvorski, 1997; Sauerland and Schenner, 2007; Koev, 2011), Korean (Chung, 2006, 2007; Lee 2011), German (Faller, 2006; Schenner, 2008), Japanese (McCready and Ogata, 2007), among others. Several diagnostics have been used to determine the semantic properties of evidentials, including whether they can be challenged and whether they embed. These diagnostics allow for an empirical classification of evidential systems across languages, establishing which properties are shared cross-linguistically and which vary.

Some of the languages do encode source of information by morphological mechanisms. Turkish, for example, marks evidentiality by morphological endings like -*dl*, which encodes the speaker's firsthand experience of the basic-level proposition conveyed in the utterance. In this language, -*mIş* encodes the speaker's indirect acquisition of the information that has been acquired and gained either through verbal communication, quotations, argumentations, or inference. All past-tense sentences involve a choice between these two suffixes, as depicted in the following examples:

1 *memet gel-dI*.
 Memet come-PAST- DIR- 3SG.
 Memet came (DIRECT).
2 *memet gel-mIş*.
 Memet come-PAST- INDIR- 3SG.
 Memet came (INDIRECT).

As these examples show, Turkish has grammaticalized and obligatory evidential devices.

Unlike Turkish, some languages, like English and Persian, lack such morpho-syntactic devices to mark evidentiality. They both mark it lexically. For instance, in English you can use sentence (3) to indicate that you are not willing to specify the exact source of information conveyed by the sentence:

3 John arrived.

But by adding some lexical items, like saw/heard/figure out, you can specify the information source in these languages, for example:

4 I **saw** that John arrived.
5 I **heard** that John has arrived.
6 I **inferred** that John had arrived, for he had left a trace of having been there.

6 Evidentiality

The same happens in Persian. In this language, lexical items index the evidentiality, too, and as such they are considered as evidentials in the following sentences:

7 man **did-am** ke 'ali resid.
   I **saw** that Ali arrived.
8 man **shenid-am** ke 'ali resid.
   I **heard** that Ali arrived.
9 man **tashxis dad-am/fahmid-am** ke 'ali resid-e ast.
   I **inferred/figured out** that Ali arrived has.
   I inferred/ figured out that Ali has arrived.

Omidvari and Golfam (2017) are the first researchers who investigated evidentiality in Persian. They believe that Persian lacks grammatical markers like affixes to indicate evidentiality. But lexical devices are used to represent evidentiality and to distinguish between direct and indirect evidentiality. They believe that direct evidentials contain observational/ visual evidentials represented by sentences, including simple present and past perceptional verbs, besides visual lexical and visual verbal items. These lexical visual items confirm that the narrator is the observer and takes the responsibility of the action described by the narrator. There are also indirect evidentials represented by direct and indirect quotations, assumptions, and inferences. Modality and aspect like impersonal passives, modals, and present perfect aspect are lexical manifestations of Persian evidentiality.

Theoretically speaking, Barnes (1984, mentioned in Habler, 2002: 156) uses a hierarchy as shown here to demonstrate the relation between different types of evidentials:

Visual > nonvisual > apparent > secondhand > assumed (direct) > (indirect) (absent)

In this hierarchical organization, Barnes locates and considered reported speech as the indirect evidential. Evidentiality considered as the linguistic process of encoding source of information has some important functions in communication and discourse. Aikhenvald (2004a) has provided the preferred evidential choices as follows:

Visual > nonvisual sensory > inferred > reported > assumed

She believes that visual evidentials are more reliable than others and they are less marked.

What are the evidentials good for? First, they are the indications of the speaker's degree of commitment to the information mentioned so that the speaker qualifies the validity of the proposition. Second, evidentiality is used to clarify a concrete perspective by specifying the details of the statement and vividness of a fact or story. Third, they are used as a form of social action to show the avoidance of being wrong, to be precise, the speaker's ability to remember the details of the information source. This is called epistemological stance; a stand speakers take on how they acquire the information, how they know it (Mushin, 2001). Fourth, they show the speaker's stance and position within the community. Aikhenvald (2018) mentioned Mamaindê as a language in which evidentiality use equals to a mechanism of face saving. In this language, the avoidance of being wrong in narration is related to the avoidance of losing face. There, evidentials provide the speaker with a way to losing face in a speech community in which one's words represent one's character.

Ifantidou (2001) believes that evidentials have two main functions: to indicate the source of knowledge and to indicate the speaker's degree of certainty about the proposition.

The theoretical framework of the present article is based on Aikhenvald (2004, 2018). There, she uses hierarchical mechanisms, described in previous paragraphs, which will be applied here, too.

Evidentiality has been viewed from a psycholinguistic perspective. Mehrabi and Mahmoodi-Bakhtiari (2019a, 2019b) have found that psycholinguistically speaking, the evidentiality hierarchy is real, and regardless of the kind of language, direct visual evidentials are processed longer than the indirect evidentials.

The main question of their inquiry (2019a) is the psycholinguistic reality of evidentiality hierarchy arranged from direct (witnessed) evidential to indirect (inferred/reported . . .) evidential. This study investigates processing of sentences containing evidentials by the cross-modal lexical decision method run by DMDX software. The theoretical framework is mainly based on episodic processing in which mental representations of linguistic items are not as abstract as they seem, but it is subject to the sensory input by which the representation is formed. The independent variable is evidential type and the dependent variable is the subjects' reaction times to the visual stimuli. Subjects were 30 university students, age 20 to 22, classified into two groups of male and female. As for the results, they show that in Persian along evidentiality hierarchy, sentences containing direct witnessed evidentials are processed later and longer than the secondhand inferred evidential, besides the fact that there is a significant difference between sensory and non-sensory/secondhand evidential. The explanation is that processing a direct evidential needs much more cortical activation for areas like memory and attention, leading to much more cognitive load than inference, which is limited just to the frontal lobe. Findings approve the psychological reality of this theoretical hierarchy in Persian, classifying which into direct/sensory and indirect/non-sensory evidentials.

Another study (2019b) investigates processing of sentences containing evidentials by the cross-modal lexical/picture decision method. The main question of this inquiry is the psycholinguistic reality of evidentiality hierarchy arranged from direct (witnessed) to indirect (inferred) evidential, too. Again, the theoretical framework is mainly based on episodic processing in which mental representations of linguistic items are not as abstract as they seem, but it is subject to the sensory input by which the representation is formed. As for the results, they show that (1) morpho-syntactic evidential encodings have no direct influence on the processing time and cognitive load; (2) both in Persian and Turkish in evidentiality hierarchy, sentences containing direct witnessed evidentials are processed later and longer than the secondhand inferred evidentials; and (3) direct speech and indirect reported speech are processed differently, in such a way that participants showed superior and faster memory for the exact wording of direct rather than indirect speech.

1.1.1 Evidentiality in languages of the world

According to Aikhenvald's typology (2004) there are two main categories of evidentiary marking:

1 Indirectivity marking ("type I")
2 Evidential marking ("type II")

The first category (indirectivity) only states if there is evidence for a certain claim; it makes no distinction between the natures of the evidence. The second type (evidential marking) describes the type of evidence (such as whether the evidence is visual, reported, or inferred).

Type I

Systems of indirectivity, or inferentiality, are widespread in Turkic and Uralic languages. These languages contrast direct information (reported directly) and indirect information (reported indirectly, focused on its reception by the speaker/recipient), indicating if there is proof for a certain source of information. Contrary to the other evidential "type II" systems, an indirectivity marking does not provide information about the knowledge's source; it makes no difference if the knowledge came from perception, inference, or hearsay. However, some Turkic languages make a distinction between reported indirect and non-reported indirect; for more information, see Johanson (2003, 2000). Turkish verbs like the following demonstrate this:

10 *gel-di*
    come-past
    "came"
11 *gel-miş*
    come-indir.past
    "obviously came, came (as far as understood)"

In the word *geldi*, the unmarked suffix *-di* indicates past tense. In the second word *gelmiş*, the suffix *-miş* also indicates past tense but *indirectly*. It may be translated into English with the added phrases *obviously*, *apparently*, or *as far as I understand*. The direct past tense marker *-di* is unmarked (or neutral) in the sense that whether or not evidence exists supporting the statement is not specified.

Type II

The other broad type of evidentiality systems ("type II") specifies the nature of the evidence supporting a statement. These kinds of evidence can be divided into such categories as:

- Witness vs. non-witness
- Firsthand vs. secondhand vs. thirdhand
- Sensory
    - Visual vs. nonvisual (i.e. auditory, olfactory, etc.)
- Inferential
- Reportative
    - Hearsay
    - Quotative
- Assumed

A *witness* evidential indicates that the information source was obtained through direct observation by the speaker. Usually this is from visual, or *eyewitness*, observation, but some languages also mark information directly heard with information directly seen. A witness evidential is usually contrasted with a *non-witness* evidential, which indicates that the information was not witnessed personally but was obtained through a secondhand source or was inferred by the speaker.

A *secondhand* evidential is used to mark any information that was not personally observed or experienced by the speaker. This may include inferences or reported information. This type of evidential may be contrasted with an evidential that indicates any other kind of source. A few languages distinguish between secondhand and thirdhand information sources.

Sensory evidentials can often be divided into different types. Some languages mark *visual* evidence differently from *nonvisual* evidence that is heard, smelled, or felt. The Kashaya language has a separate *auditory* evidential.

An *inferential* evidential indicates information was not personally experienced but was inferred from indirect evidence. Some languages have different types of inferential evidentials. Some of the inferentials found indicate:

1 Information inferred by direct physical evidence
2 Information inferred by general knowledge
3 Information inferred/assumed because of speaker's experience with similar situations
4 Past deferred realization

In many cases, different inferential evidentials also indicate epistemic modality, such as uncertainty or probability. For example, one evidential may indicate that the information is inferred but of uncertain validity, while another indicates that the information is inferred but unlikely to be true.

Reportative evidentials indicate that the information was reported to the speaker by another person.

A few languages distinguish between *hearsay* evidentials and *quotative* evidentials. Hearsay indicates reported information that may or may not be accurate. A quotative indicates the information is accurate and not open to interpretation, that is, is a direct quotation. An example of a reportative from Shipibo (*-ronki*):

12 *Aronkiai.*
    *a-:*do- **ronki-:reprt-** *ai:* incompl
    "It is said that she will do it."/"She says that she will do it."

All languages have some way(s) to identify the information's original source. European languages (such as Germanic and Romance languages) often indicate evidential-type information through modal verbs (Spanish: *deber de*, Dutch: *zouden*, Danish: *skulle*, German: *sollen*) or other lexical words (like adverbials in English: reportedly) or phrases (English: *it seems to me*). Some languages have a specific type of evidentiality that must always be conveyed grammatically. The elements used to indicate the information source in European languages are optional, and they typically do not serve as indicators of evidentiality as their primary role, hence they do not constitute a grammatical category. "As I hear," "as I can see," "as far as I understand," "they say," "it is said," "it seems," "it seems to me that," "it looks like," "it appears that," "it turns out that," "alleged," "stated," "allegedly," "reportedly," "obviously," and so on are all acceptable translations of the necessary components of grammatical evidentiality systems into English.

According to Alexandra Aikhenvald (2004), grammatical evidentiality is present in around a quarter of the world's languages. She adds that, to her knowledge, no studies on grammatical evidentiality in sign languages have been done.

Depending on the language, grammatical evidentiality can take on several forms, such as affixes, clitics, or particles. For instance, Japanese has grammaticalized nouns and inferential evidentials that are realized as suffixes on a variety of primarily verbal predicates. As another instance, the verbs in the Eastern Pomo language have the suffixes -ink'e (nonvisual sensory), -ine (inferential), -le (hearsay), and -ya (direct knowledge).

In languages where evidentiality is not distinguished from epistemic modality, the use of evidentiality has pragmatic implications. A person who makes a false statement that is qualified as a belief, for instance, might be seen to be wrong; a person who makes a false statement that is qualified as a personally observed fact, on the other hand, is likely to be thought to have lied.

Given that it can be represented in a variety of ways and is always optional, evidentiality is not regarded as a grammatical category in English. Contrarily, several other languages (such as Quechua, Aymara, and Yukaghir) demand that the speaker indicate whether the main verb or the entire phrase is evidence, or they provide a choice of affixes for indirect evidence, with direct experience being the assumed mode of evidence by default.

Consider these English sentences:

I am famished.
John is famished.

We are unlikely to say the second unless someone (perhaps John himself) has told us that John is extremely hungry. (We might still say it for someone incapable of speaking for themselves, such as a baby or a pet.) If we are simply assuming that John is hungry based on the way he looks or acts, we are more likely to say something like:

John <u>looks</u> famished.
John <u>seems</u> famished.

John <u>would be</u> famished by now.
John <u>must be</u> famished by now.

Here, the fact that we are relying on sensory evidence, rather than direct experience, is conveyed by our use of the word *looks* or *seems*.

Another situation in which the evidential modality is expressed in English is in certain kinds of predictions, namely, those based on the evidence at hand. These can be referred to as "predictions with evidence." For example:

Look at those clouds! It's **going to** rain! (Compare "It will rain!")

Some languages are borderline cases. For example, French is mostly like English in not having grammatical evidentiality, but does allow some ability to express it via inflection. By using the <u>conditional mood</u>—which has three uses: conditions, future-in-the-past, and hearsay—journalistic French frequently makes a distinction between *Il a reconnu sa culpabilité* and *Il aurait reconnu sa culpabilité*. Both translate to "He has admitted his guilt," but with an implication of certainty with the first, and the idea of "reportedly" with the second. The same happens in Spanish: *Él ha reconocido su culpa* vs. *Él habría reconocido su culpa*. It also happens in Portuguese: *Ele reconheceu sua culpa* vs. *Ele teria reconhecido sua culpa*.

Terms such as evidential, inferential, indirective, mediative, and epistemic are all used by different scholars to describe evidentiality in Persian. For instance, Jahani (2000) adopts the term "indirectivity" from Johanson (1996) to refer to indirect knowledge, which in its turn can be either reportative (information obtained through the report of another person) or inferential (information obtained through drawing conclusions), as opposed to direct (self-experienced) knowledge. The question of whether a grammatical category of "indirective" exists in written Modern Persian is dealt with in several articles by Gernot Windfuhr (1982) and Gilbert Lazard (1985). Windfuhr (1982: 285) concludes that "the function of the inferential forms differs from that of the direct forms in what appears to be a category of perspective, or deixis, allowing the speaker to remove himself from direct responsibility for the truth of an event." The only mention of the colloquial language in the discussion of indirectivity in Persian is found in Gernot Windfuhr's description of Persian in *The World's Major Languages*. He makes a distinction between the "literary register" and the "colloquial language" (Windfuhr, 1987: 537), stating that the verb forms that he has described as "inferential" in earlier works "express remote past in the literary register" but that "they are not confined to literary style, but are as frequent in the colloquial language without referring to remote past. What they

express is the category of inference, that is mainly second-hand knowledge, conclusion and reminiscence."
The study of Omidvari and Golfam (2017) also shows that there aren't any grammatical evidentials in Persian and like the other Indo-European languages, Persian has linguistic items that fulfill evidential function in addition to their first roles in language. Some of the evidential structures in Persian include impersonal passive forms, modal expressions, tense-aspect features, reports and quotations, and sensory and perception verbs. These formal structures include semantic frames of direct and indirect evidentiality and determine the main source of information. In New Persian there are some linguistic indicators for marking evidentiality, some of which are lexical and some others are syntactic. In the following example, some verbs of seeing encode firsthand direct evidentiality (Omidvari and Golfam, 2017: 92):

(13). *dar dam **didam** ke Beygmahammad ruye asb tāb xord.*
Immediately saw- I that Beygmohammad on horse swung.
I saw immediately that Beygmohammad swung on the horse.

Verbs of hearing encode indirect evidentiality, especially when used with perfect aspect as in (14) cited (ibid., 93):

(14). ***shenide-am*** *barāye khodat hokumat dorost karde-i.*
Have heard- I for yourself government have established- you.
I have heard that you have established a government for yourself.

In New Persian, tense and aspect conveys indirect (secondhand) evidentiality so that imperfect aspects refers to firsthand/direct source of information. Here is an example based on Omidvari and Golfam (ibid., 87 cited from Aikhenvald, 2004: 114–115):

*tuye xāne-ye mā ke kār **mikard***
In house—PRON:1Pl SUB work do: IMPF:3sg,
hamiše sheʻr **mixānd**
always poetry recite: IMPF: 3sg
boland boland **mixānde-ast**
loudly loudly recite: PERF. CONT: 3sg

In this example the first part of the sentence, which contains the past tense, shows that the speaker has witnessed the scene, but the second part of the sentence, containing present perfect, shows that the speaker has been told about the situation and the speaker has not witnessed the scene of reciting poetry loudly.

Next, (3a) conveys direct witnessed evidentials through past tense and imperfect aspect as opposed to (3b), which shows indirect evidential based on deduction or surrounding evidences or assumptions:

(3) a. *diruz dar jādde tasādof-e badi shod.*
Yesterday on road accident bad took place.
There took place a terrible accident on the road.
b. *diruz dar jādde tasādof-e badi shode ast.*
Yesterday on road accident bad has taken place.
There has taken place a terrible accident on the road.

As an example for impersonal passives you can take a look at example (4):

(4). *miguyand in āqāye Talxābādi pul pāsh midahad.*
They say this Mr. Talxābādi money for it pays.
It is said that Mr. Talxābādi pays for it. (ibid., 90)

Also modality can convey indirect evidentiality as here subjunctive mode does:

(7). *agar diruz ba'd az zohr rāh oftāde bāshand, dishab bāyad miresidand.*
If yesterday afternoon have set out- they last night must arrived- they.
If they have set out yesterday afternoon, they should have arrived by last night.
(8). *otomobil bāyād az jānebe robāyandegān ferestāde shode bāshad.*
Car must from kidnappers sent has been.
The car must have been sent by the kidnappers.

Here the subjunctive mode depicts the feeling of uncertainty and making assumption.

It should be mentioned that in Persian, as in many other languages, direct reported speech is among the most valid type of evidential, as can be seen in example (16):

(16). *Baha'edin xoramshāhi dar ebtedāye sohbat hā-ye xod ezhār dāsht: "man in ketāb rā jāme' midānam."*
Baha'edin xoramshāhi at the beginning of lecture himself said: "I this book complete consider."
At the beginning of his lecture Baha'edin xoramshāhi said: "I consider this book comprehensive."

If a grammaticalization of "indirectivity" requires that these forms be consistently used to denote "indirect" evidence, and used only in such contexts, it is, however, hard to motivate the establishment of indirectivity as a grammatical category in spoken Modern Persian. "Perfects" often get more or less clear readings of indirective evidentiality. This is the case even in reported speech.

Maryam	be man mige	ke vaqti ke	dāshte
Maryam	to I she says	That when	she has had
bā telefon	harf mizade	yedafe sedā qat' shode	
with telephone	was talking	suddenly voice cut has become	

"Mariam tells me that when she was speaking on the phone suddenly the sound was cut."

The use of *dāshte harf mizade* as opposed to *dāsht harf mizad* in the preceding example would indicate that the speaker doubts the validity of what he reports. If the progressive form *dāshte mikarde* is found only in reported speech, it is possible to explain this form also as post-terminal, since the person speaking has not witnessed the progress of the action himself; he only reports it as an ongoing action after its completion (Jahani, 2000: 203).

1.2 Evidentiality in literature

So far there has not been any research done by considering evidentiality as a stylistic strategy in general and in Persian literature, in particular—especially as a means to analyze the great works of literature, namely masterpieces, though this kind of analysis can reveal some stylistic peculiarities of great writers/poets in terms of the degree of certainty of their narratives. This investigation is among the first of those attempts.

Black (2006: 53) believes that

> Narrative is a basic human activity. We all tell stories—to ourselves, to others. First person narratives are commonplace, from pub conversations to parents telling children about their past. ... So the basic types of narration which are considered here are, very nearly, as old as the human race itself.

Literature is no exception to this common phenomenon, if we account literary works as narrations of stories or even internal world ecology, feeling, and atmosphere.

Reference list

Aikhenvald, A. (2004). *Evidentiality*. Oxford: Oxford University Press.
Aikhenvald, A. (2018). Evidentiality: The framework. In A. Aikhenvald (ed.), *Oxford Handbook of Evidentiality*. Oxford: Oxford University Press.
Barnes, J. (1984). Evidentials in the Tuyuca verb. *International Journal of American Linguistics* 50: 255–271.
Black, E. (2006). *Pragmatic Stylistics*. Edinburgh: Edinburgh University Press.
Chung, K. S. (2006). Korean evidentials and assertion. In D. Baumer, D Montero & M. Scanlon (eds.), *Proceedings of the 25th West Coast Conference on Formal Linguistics*. Somerville, MA: Cascadilla Proceedings Project. (pp. 105–113).
Chung, K. S. (2007). Spatial-deictic tense and evidentials in Korean. *Natural Language Semantics* 153(3): 187–219.
Faller, M. (2006). *Evidentiality Above and Below Speech Acts*. Ms. http://semanticsarchive.net/Archive/GZiZjBhO/.
Habler, G. (2002). Evidentiality and reported speech in Romance languages. In T. Güldemann & M. von Roncador (eds.), *Reported Discourse: A Meeting Ground for Different Linguistic Domains*. Amsterdam: John Benjamins Publishing Company.
Ifantidou, E. (2001). *Evidentials and Relevance*. Amsterdam: John Benjamins Publishing Company.
Izvorski, R. (1997). The present perfect as an epistemic modal. In A. Lawson (ed.), *Proceedings from Semantics and Linguistic Theory VII*. Ithaca, NY: Cornell University. (pp. 222–239).
Jahani, C. (2000). Expression of indirectivity in spoken Modern Persian. In L. Johanson & B. Utas (eds.), *Evidentials: Turkic, Iranian and Neighbouring Languages*. Berlin: Mouton de Gruyter.
Johanson, L. (1996). On Bulgarian and Turkic indirectives. In N. Boretzky, W. Enninger & T. Stolz (eds.), *Areale, Kontakte, Dialekte. Sprache und ihre Dynamik in mehrsprachigen Situationen*. (Bochum-Essener Beiträge zur Sprachwandelforschung 24.). Bochum: Brockmeyer. (pp. 84–94).
Johanson, L. (2000). Turkic indirectives. In L. Johanson & B. Utas (eds.), *Evidentials: Turkic, Iranian and Neighbouring Languages*. Berlin: Mouton de Gruyter. (pp. 61–87).
Johanson, L. (2003). Evidentiality in Turkic. In A. Y. Aikhenvald & R. M. W. Dixon (eds.), *Studies in Evidentiality*. Amsterdam: John Benjamins Publishing Company. (pp. 273–290).
Johnson, M. K. (1988). Discriminating the origin of information. In T. F. Oltmanns & B. A. Maher (eds.), *Delusional Beliefs*. New York: Wiley. (pp. 34–65).
Johnson, M. K., S. Hashtroudi and D. S. Lindsay. (1993). Source monitoring. *Psychological Bulletin* 114: 3–28.
Koev, T. (2011). Evidentiality and temporal distance learning. In N. Ashton, A. Chereches & D. Lutz (eds.), *Proceedings from Semantics and Linguistic Theory(SALT) XXI*. Ithaca, NY: CLC Publications. (pp. 115–134).
Lazard, G. (1985). L'inférentiel ou passé distancié en persan. *Studia Iranica* 14: 27–42.

Lee, J. (2011). *Evidentiality and Its Interaction with Tense: Evidence from Korean.* The Ohio State University dissertation.

McCready, E. and N. Ogata. (2007). Evidentiality, modality and probability. *Linguistics and Philosophy* 30(2): 147–206.

Mehrabi, M. and B. Mahmoodi-Bakhtiari. (2019a/1398a). The psychological reality of evidentiality hierarchy in Persian during sentence listening comprehension. *Language Related Research* (in Press).

Mehrabi, M. and B. Mahmoodi-Bakhtiari. (2019b/1398b). A comparative study of evidentiality auditory comprehension of Persian, Turkish, and English. *Journal of Comparative Linguistic Researches* (in Press).

Morady Moghaddam, M. (2019). *The Praxis of Indirect Reports Cognitive, Ciopragmatic, and Philosophical Issues.* Switzerland: Springer Nature.

Murray, S. (2017). *The Semantics of Evidentials.* Oxford: Oxford University Press.

Mushin, I. (2001). *Evidentiality and Epistemological Stance.* Narrative Retelling. Amsterdam: John Benjamins Publishing Company.

Omidvari, A. and A. Golfam. (2017). Investigating evidentiality in Persian: A typological approach. *Jostarhaye Zabani (Language Researches).* Vol. 36. (pp. 79–99). Tehran: Tarbiyat Moddares University.

Sauerland, U. and M. Schenner. (2007). Embedded evidentials in Bulgarian. In P. W. Estela (ed.), *Proceedings of Sinn und Bedeutung 11.* Barcelona: Universitat Pompeu Fabra. (pp. 525–539).

Schenner, M. (2008). Double face evidentials in German. In AlteGronn (ed.), *Proceedings of Sinn und Bedeutung 12.* Oslo, Norway: ILOS. (pp. 552–566).

Unal, E. (2018). Evidentials, information source, and cognition. In A. Aikhenvald (ed.), *Oxford Handbook of Evidentiality.* Oxford: Oxford University Press.

Windfuhr, G. L. (1982). The verbal category of inference in Persian. In *Monumentům Georg Morgenstierne II.* (Acta Iranica 22.). Leiden: E. G. Brill. (pp. 263–287).

Windfuhr, G. L. (1987). Persian, in Comrie, B. (ed.), *The World's Major Languages.* London: Routledge. (pp. 523–546).

2 Theoretical considerations

2.1 Evidentiality as a pragmatic device

Pragmatics is the aspect of the study of language in use. It is concerned with how language users interact, communicate, and interpret linguistic behaviors. Meanwhile, literary stylistics is the study of how close attention to language use can contribute to accounts of how texts are understood and evaluated. Yet despite the apparent overlaps and commonalities of interest between the two disciplines, there has, until now, been relatively little work that brings them together, or that explores the interface between them. This interface is central to "pragmatic" literary stylistics. Pragmatic literary stylistics is developing within the framework of a broader range of work, which has been termed the "cognitive humanities" to use Chapman and Clark (2014: 1) terminology.

Theoretically speaking, reported speech is classified as a kind of indirect evidential (Omidvari and Golfam, 2017: 79 and Habler, 2002), evidentiality being considered as the linguistic process of encoding the source of information, which is mainly opaque and must be interpreted according to context and contextual factors. That is why we have discussed the theoretical considerations of reported speech. Another reason for mentioning such a topic here is that reported speech has been frequently used in Sa'di's narrative style.

2.1.1 Reported speech

The prime motivation for the use of direct discourse is that it seems to allow the reader direct contact with the character (Black, 2006: 70). Leech and Short argue that while the norm for reporting speech is direct discourse, the norm for reporting thought is indirect thought, because thoughts are not known to anyone but the thinker (outside of fictions). In addition, they need not be verbalized, so indirect thought, which is essentially the

DOI: 10.4324/9781003371786-3

Theoretical considerations 19

narrator's verbalization of a character's thoughts, must be regarded as the norm (ibid., 69).

In the former traditional approaches to grammar, there has been a distinction between direct and indirect reported speech. But here the functional aspect of reported speech is of interest. Barnes (1984, mentioned in Habler, 2002: 156) uses a hierarchy to demonstrate the relation between different types of evidentials:

visual > nonvisual > apparent > secondhand > assumed (direct) > (indirect) (absent)

In this hierarchical organization, Barnes locates and considered reported speech as the indirect evidentials. Authors like Capone (2019: 3, 2016: 55) believe that reported speech, whether direct or indirect, is opaque semantically and pragmatically, for both the production and comprehension of them needs encoding and decoding of contextual and pragmatic information. So comprehension and production of these kinds of evidentials needs a large amount of contextual information; that's why Capone calls them opaque. Here, the question is which kind of contextual and pragmatic information is needed for the appropriate use of this linguistic mechanism in terms of production and comprehension. To answer such a question first requires and explanation of the semantic and grammatical structure of reported speech, in general and in Persian, in particular. Here, the focus is on the ways in which they are used and the contribution they make to give fictional discourse the complex layers of meaning and implicatures that they can generate. They are an important means of characterization.

Functional approach

Wierzbicka)1974 cited in Coulmus, 1986: 30) adopted the first functional approach to the study of reported speech. She believes that direct speech has a theatrical nature; in direct speech, the reporter-speaker plays the role of the reported/original speaker.

Li (1986), following Haiman and Thompson (1984) and Givön (1980), points out some results about the functional and semantic differences of direct and indirect speech. Here again the concepts of reported and reporter speaker are used. But in indirect speech, the reporter-speaker does not play the role of the reported speaker (ibid.).

Li believes that reporter speaker is representing the reported speaker in form, t, nonverbals, and content in direct speech, but in indirect speech the form and the nonverbal messages of the reported speech belong to the reporter-speaker. The reporter-speaker intends for the hearer to believe that only the content of the reported speech originates from the reported speaker. Li (ibid.) brings some evidences to persuade the reader to believe in a functional approach to reported speech including:

1 Direct speech is a language universal rooted in basic human cognitive abilities like reproduction and mimicking.
2 There will be found some cultural explanations for the absence of indirect speech in languages like Amharic, Nanaja, and Paez. In Paez, for example, you are not allowed to take the responsibility of the other's speech.
3 There is an interconnection between reported speech and evidentiality in such a way that the functional approaches taken by evidentiality can be adopted here too.

Coulmus (1986: 30) believes in cultural considerations and reasons about the functional differences between direct and indirect speech. He says that in all the languages the reporter speaker is taking the perspective of the reported/original speaker in direct speeches, while in indirect speech the reporter speaker can manipulate the reported speaker's message based on his/her own linguistic and encyclopedic knowledge. He believes that although direct speech is much more authentic than indirect speech, by adding comments—like "that is exactly what he said," "these are his own exact words," "the words which he used were these," this is his/her exact wording"—to the indirect speech, the degree of authenticity can change.

Thompson (1996), adopting a systemic functional approach to reported speech, maintains that the classification of reported speech into just two broad categories is inadequate for explanation of this functional linguistic topic; "the voices in the texts" must be investigated instead. What Thompson means by "voices" is the linguistic traces left back signaling that there are other(s)' voices in the text. Such a linguistic strategy is used in Persian by words that can be considered as lexical markers of indirect speech, words like "argument, advice, reply, claim, result, decision, explanation, suggestion, threat, promise, persuade, observation, order, investigation, warning" and so on.

Cultural-cognitive approach

Goddard and Wierzbicka (2019: 198) believe that direct speech is a semantic universal. They maintain that:

> First, all languages appear to have resources for quoting other people's speech. What we mean by this is that all languages have a word (a

Theoretical considerations 21

verb) encoding, in one of its meanings, the indefinable concept SAY, with a valency option which allows this word to introduce a quotation: "he/she said:—"; and this basic frame can be extended to include an addressee: "he/she said to someone:—." Second, all languages appear to have resources for approximating other people's speech, that is, they allow the verb meaning SAY (or SPEAK) to combine with a phrase (or a word) meaning "like this," i.e. in the frame "he/she said/spoke like this . . . ." Third, all languages appear to allow the verb meaning SAY to be used in the frame "I say to you," followed by some other words, perhaps for the purpose of drawing someone's special attention to what the speaker is saying. Beyond these commonalities (and a few others, which can't be discussed here), there is a great deal of cross-linguistic diversity, often emblematic of cultural diversity.

They (ibid.:191) have used some instances from Goemai language in which there is no direct speech superficially, but considered more carefully, there are some other linguistic strategies like applying logophoric pronouns to indicate the existence of such a direct speech whose vivid appearance is restricted by sociocultural considerations. For example:

(87) (b) *Yàm-nùùn Gòelóng yóól/ wúl.*
"The brother of Goelong rose (and) arrived. (He$_1$ said to himself) he$_1$ goes (and) sees his$_1$ sister's child."

This example shows that according to the gloss, the man, in his own thoughts, refers to himself as "he" (or, more precisely, as "he$_1$"). This seems to us entirely implausible. Here is our own proposed gloss: "The brother of Goelong rose (and) arrived. He said to himself: I will go (and) see my sister's child." The idea that logophoric reporting of speech may seem strange and implausible to speakers of European languages, but in West African languages, it may be entirely plausible, given the cultural importance of "triadic communication." The use of intermediaries in West Africa to channel information between an addressor and an addressee in communicative interaction is well documented in the ethnographic literature and is evident to the most casual observer.

Bernárdez (2017) develops a view of evidentiality based on cultural linguistics. He notes that, in the past, some accounts of evidentiality have ignored language use, only keeping an account of grammatical and/or lexical elements, in isolation from context. Bernárdez reviews several definitions of evidentiality, presenting examples from a large and diverse sample of languages. He argues that evidentials are more likely to arise in groups that conceptualize themselves as small groups and live in isolated environments, finding the world around themselves as difficult to access (due to impenetrability, weather conditions, or absence of literacy), and their relations either within the group or with neighboring groups are very tight. He then presents a set of culturally constructed principles that appear to be at work in association with the evidentials in all the languages referred to, including the principle that "every member of the community knows—to a greater or lesser degree—all, or most other members" (Bernárdez, 2017: 454). Overall, Bernárdez (ibid.: 455) shows how it is "possible and convenient indeed to try to interpret evidentiality in the framework of cultural linguistics as driven by cultural and cognitive factors and through history." The analyses of evidentiality and reported speech in these studies make another case for the potential of cultural considerations in linguistics when examining cultural conceptualizations that are encoded in the morpho-syntactic and lexical features of human languages.

Reported speech structure in Persian

Yousef and Torabi (2018: 312–319) offer a general overview of Persian reported (indirect) speech grammatically. But what is of importance here can be mentioned as follows:

1. In Persian it is the tense of the "reporting verb" that determines what tense you should use—it is rather the tense of the verb in the *original* sentence, as you think it was *originally* said. After the reporting verb, you need *ke* ("that"), which, as in English, can be dropped. Similar to English, there can be changes in adverbs—like the change from *injā* ("here") to *ānjā* ("there") and the like.
2. When reporting statements that originally used past tense, then not a backshift of tenses (as in English) but a *change* of tenses would be necessary—and this again is regardless of the tense of the reporting verb that starts the sentence. The following instances elaborate on the topic:

    a) <u>Simple present/past</u>:

    minā: "be ānjā raftam."
    minā mi-guyad/goft [ke] be ānjā rafte [ast]
    Mina: "I went there."→ Mina says/said (that) she has gone there.

    b) <u>Past progressive</u>:

    minā: "be ānjā mi-raftam."
    minā mi-guyad/goft [ke] be ānjā mi-rafte [ast]
    Mina: "I was going there."→ Mina says/said (that) she had been going there.

c) Past perfect:

minā: "be ānjā rafte budam."
minā mi-guyad/goft [ke] be ānjā rafte bude
Mina says/said (that) she had gone there.

d) Past perfect progressive:

minā: "mi-tavāneste budam bā kas-e digari ezdevāj konam."
minā mi-guyad/goft [ke] mi-tavāneste bude ast bā kas-e digari ezdevāj konad
Mina says/said (that) she could have married someone else.

3 *Imperative* is only possible in *direct speech*; in reported speech, it has to change to the subjunctive. *Subjunctive* has no tense to change; it remains unchanged. No change of tense is required for *conditionals* and *wishes*.

Functions of reported speech

The theoretical framework used here is the functionalistic approach, which Capone (2016, 2019) takes toward the study of reported speech besides cultural linguistic approach to the study of the linguistic phenomenon of evidentiality Bernardez (2017) adopted based on Sharifian (2015a, 2017). Capone maintains that both direct and indirect speech is opaque pragmatically, but the indirect speech is much more opaque than the other because the indirect speech is the reporter speaker's mental representation of the mental representation of the reported speaker. This mental representation is largely influenced by contextual factors. Adapting cultural linguistic theoretical framework, it can best be shown how the concept of "trust" can be conceptualized in Persian by linguistic strategy of reported speech.

Morady Moghaddam (2019: 192–195) attributes some social and pragmatic aspects to reported speech in Persian: phatic, informative, expressive, aesthetic, and directive functions. He believes that Persian reported speech puts emphasis on someone's previous speech, so it can help individuals start a conversation and keep communication lines open. Second, by paraphrasing, Persian speakers use reported speech to provide new information that relies on truth and value sets. Third, Persian speakers use reported speech to express their feeling and attitudes. The speaker's state of mind and subjective attitudes influence the state of their speech. Fourth, Persian speakers use quotations (quoted expressions) aesthetically, which they call *Hadith* or *naghl-e ghol*, which are the fixed expressions from the authorities applied in order to add flavor to their speech. Fifth, as he puts it:

24 *Theoretical considerations*

> Reported speech is a powerful device for influencing the attitudes and/ or behavior of others. Here, the illocutionary force of the reported speech requires the hearer to act accordingly. In addition, the voice of others, which is included in the reported speech, empowers the reporter to take control of the situation.
>
> Morady Moghaddam (2019: 194)

Conceptualizing "social trust"

Morady Moghaddam (2019: 159) sees a close relation between indirect speech and the socio-cognitive concept of trust in Persian:

> Indirect reporting is a social phenomenon that is fundamentally a risk-taking process. The original speaker must take risks and trust the reporter as a faithful transformer of the source information. On the other hand, the reporter must trust the original speaker as a trustworthy source of information. In other words, when the reporter bases his/her report on the information emitted by the original speaker, it shows that the reporter trusts the original speaker as an authority (or at least decides that trusting is the best alternative at the time). In addition, the reporter must also trust the hearer as a trustworthy person with whom to share information, that is, as a faithful analyzer and transformer of the reporter's utterances. The hearer must also trust the reporter as a genuine agent who is reliable enough to be taken seriously. The perlocutionary effect of the reporter's utterance depends on the degree of trustworthiness shared between the hearer and the reporter.

Moreover, Bernardez (2017) investigates into some of the languages with obligatorily complicated systems of evidentiality. After precise research, he came to this idea that paralinguistic factors (like what follow) can develop first and then preserve evidential systems in those languages:

1 The possibility of developing a linguistic evidential system is much more likely in a small linguistic community and small social groups, mainly living in isolated areas.
2 Difficulty in accessibility to the surrounding world and impenetrability of the living environment can lead to the development of evidential systems in such languages. Even the illiteracy of the native speakers can be considered as an effective factor. The former case (environmental impenetrability) is found in Chachi and the latter (illiteracy) in Quechua.
3 Close social relations between members of small speech communities and neighboring areas can lead to the possibility of evidentiality development.

Bernardez describes the third factor by the use of the concept "social trust," which he has adapted from Wierzbicka (2015). She relates the evidentiality system in general and reported speech in particular to the concept of scripts. If somebody doesn't know something—while there is no direct way for him to know that—and he wants to know it, he must ask other(s) to inform him. If he lives in a small speech community in which there is much more mutual social trust between the members, telling the truth honestly is the main communicative principle. This leads to this event that even though the asked person doesn't know the answer directly, he/she will encode the information source linguistically in some sort of evidentiality, according to Bernardez (2017: 454). So Bernardez considers some social, historical, and geographical factors as the significant reasons of the evidentiality development in these languages.

In this part of the research, we have greatly benefited from the concept of social trust as a variable to illustrate which factors affect the manner and frequency of reported speech occurrence in Persian speakers. As proved empirically by Wheeless and Grotz (1997), there is a direct relation between trust and self-disclosure. Here, again, the presupposition is that when somebody experiences feelings of trust, self-disclosure leads to the use of much indirect speech paving the ground for interpretation.

2.2 Evidentiality as a stylistic device

Stylistics is an interdisciplinary attempt that tries to apply ideas from linguistics to the study of how texts are produced, understood, and evaluated, and in addressing theoretical questions associated with this it is applicable. It necessarily has many branches, both because of the wide range of genres, modes, and purposes of the texts that are the object of study for stylistics, and because of the variety of frameworks from linguistics within which they can be analyzed. Pragmatic literary stylistics is one such branch. Of course, not all pragmatic stylistics focuses on literary texts, and not all literary stylistics applies ideas from pragmatics. The theoretical and analytical tools of stylistics in general and of pragmatic stylistics in particular can be applied to any kind of text. Literary texts, meanwhile, can be discussed in relation to a wide range of descriptive and analytical tools developed in linguistics, for instance, evidentiality.

2.2.1 The definition of style

Hogan (2014: 518) characterizes style as "distinctive linguistic expression" and stylistics as "the analysis" of such expression "and the description of its purpose and effect." Boyd (2017) believes that "cognitive neuroscientists have recently emphasized that minds work as pattern extractors that in

Theoretical considerations

Gerald Edelman's words, "the 'primary mode' of thought is 'pattern recognition'" and that human minds in particular are hierarchical pattern extractors (Kurzweil, 2012) with a special appetite for novel pattern (Bor, 2012). In my own recent work, I suggest that we need to see writing and composing a work of art and literature as cognitive play with pattern.

One of the exciting recent developments in stylistics is the use of the tools and methodologies of corpus linguistics to teach and perform what is called corpus stylistics (Hardy, 2007: 79).

We think Firth is right when he considers that:

> Our brains build models of the world and continuously modify these models on the basis of the signals that reach our senses. So, what we actually perceive are our brain's models of the world. They are not the world itself, but, for us, they are as good as. You could say that our perceptions are fantasies that coincide with reality.
>
> (Frith, 2009: 134–135)

Meanwhile, every author uses a special technique to form and fabricate his own fantasies. These forming techniques are called his style.

Shen (2014: 193) defines style and distinguishes it from narrative in this way: "style" refers to how the content is presented and "narrative discourse" to how the story is told. From these definitions, we may derive the following equation:

Style = Language = Technique = Discourse

Mason (2014: 182) also considers a cognitive turn in postclassical narratology, classical being related to structural paradigm in narrative analysis. In the cognitive turn fields such as cognitive poetics have historically borrowed substantively enough from the cognitive disciplines like cognitive linguistics to explain how literary works are produced and perceived.

Reference list

Barnes, J. (1984). Evidentials in the Tuyuca verb. *International Journal of American Linguistics* 50: 255–271.
Bernardez, E. (2017). Evidentiality—A cultural interpretation. In F. Sharifian (ed.), *Advances in Cultural Linguistics*. Singapore: Springer. (pp. 433–459).
Black, E. (2006). *Pragmatic Stylistics*. Edinburgh: Edinburgh University Press.
Bor, D. (2012). *The Ravenous Brain: How the New Science of Consciousness Explains Our Insatiable Search for Meaning*. New York: Basic Books.

Theoretical considerations 27

Boyd, B. (2017). Patterns of thought. In M. Burke & E. T. Troscianko (eds.), *Cognitive Literary Science Dialogues between Literature and Cognition*. Oxford: Oxford University Press.

Capone, A. (2016). *The Pragmatics of Indirect Reports: Socio-philosophical Considerations*. Barcelona: Springer.

Capone, A. (2019). On the social praxis of indirect reporting. In A. Capone et al. (eds.), *Indirect Reports and Pragmatics in the World Languages*. Switzerland: Springer.

Chapman, S. and B. Clark. (2014). *Pragmatic Literary Stylistics*. London: Palgrave.

Coulmus, F. (1986). Reported speech: Some general issues. In F. Coulmas (ed.), *Direct and Indirect Speech*. Berlin: Mouton de Gruyter.

Frith, C. (2009). *Making Up the Mind: How the Brain Creates Our Mental World*. Hoboken, NJ: Wiley Blackwell.

Givön, T. (1980). The binding hierarchy and the typology of complements. *Studies in Language* 4(3): 333–377.

Goddard, C. and A. Wierzbicka. (2019). Direct and indirect speech revisited: Semantic universals and semantic diversity. In A. Capone et al. (eds.), *Indirect Reports and Pragmatics in the World Languages*. Switzerland: Springer.

Habler, G. (2002). Evidentiality and reported speech in Romance languages. In T. Güldemann & M. von Roncador (eds.), *Reported Discourse: A meeting Ground for Different Linguistic domains*. Amsterdam: John Benjamins Publishing Company.

Haiman, J. and S. A. Thompson. (1984). 'Subordination' in universal grammar. *Proceedings from the 10th Annual Meeting of the Berkeley Linguistics Society*. Berkeley: University of California Press, (pp. 510–523).

Hardy, D. E. (2007). Corpus stylistics as a discovery procedure. In G. Watson & S. Zyngier (eds.), *Literature and Stylistics for Language Learners Theory and Practice*. London: Palgrave.

Hogan, P. C. (2014). Stylistics, emotions, and neuroscience. In M. Burke (ed.), *The Routledge Handbook of Stylistics*. London: Routledge.

Kurzweil, R. (2012). *How to Create a Mind: The Secret of Human Thought Revealed*. London: Viking.

Li, N. C. (1986). Direct and indirect speech: A functional study. In F. Coulmas (ed.), *Direct and Indirect Speech*. Berlin: Mouton de Gruyter. (pp. 29–46).

Omidvari, A. and A. Golfam. (2017). Investigating evidentiality in Persian: A typological approach. *Jostār-hā ye Zabāni (Language Related Researches)*. Vol. 36. (pp. 79–99).

Mason, J. (2014). Narrative. In P. Stockwell & S. Whiteley (eds.), *The Cambridge Handbook of Stylistics*. London: Cambridge.

Morady Moghaddam, M. (2019). *The Praxis of Indirect Reports Cognitive, Ciopragmatic, and Philosophical Issues*. Switzerland: Springer Nature.

Sharifian, F. (2015a). Cultural linguistics. In F. Sharifian (ed.), *The Routledge Handbook of Language and Culture*. London: Routledge. (pp. 473–492).

Sharifian, F. (2017). *Cultural Linguistics*. Amsterdam: John Benjamins Publishing Company.

Shen, D. (2014). Stylistics and narratology. In M. Burke (ed.), *The Routledge Handbook of Stylistics*. London: Routledge.

Thompson, G. (1996). Voices in the text: Discourse perspectives on language reports. *Applied Linguistics* 17(4): 501–530.
Yousef, S. and H. Torabi. (2018). *Persian: A Comprehensive Grammar*. London: Routledge.
Wheeless, L. and J. Grotz. (1997). The measurement of trust and its relationship to self- disclosure. *Human Communication Research* 3(3): 250–257.
Wierzbicka, A. (1974). The semantics of direct and indirect discourse. *Papers in Linguistics* 7(3/4): 267–307.
Wierzbicka, A. (2015). Language and cultural scripts. In F. Sharifian (ed.), *Advances in Cultural Linguistics*. Singapore: Springer. (pp. 339–356).

3 Evidentiality in Sa'dī's masterpieces

INTRODUCTION

Mahlberg (2016, p. 139) introduces corpus stylistics in this way:

> Corpus stylistics employs methods from corpus linguistics to study literary texts. These methods are computer-assisted and enable the retrieval and quantification of linguistic phenomena in electronic texts. The terms "corpus stylistics" has only become popular over the past decade, although computer-assisted studies of literary texts have a long tradition spanning different fields. The objects of study in corpus stylistics are literary texts. A literary text can be seen both as an example of language and as a work of art, so it can be the basis for linguistic description as well as literary appreciation.

Analysis of data is the main mechanism for explanations represented at the end of the book. Frequency of occurrence is here adapted and applied as the main mechanism in content analysis introduced by Krippendoff (2004). It concerns the number of times an incident occurs. Here, the analysis of data from the mentioned masterpieces is mainly based on the frequency of occurrence of evidentials.

3.1 *Būstān (Sa'dī, 1396a)*

Table 3.1 shows evidential frequency in the first chapter of *Būstān* called "on justice, equity, and administration of government," which contains 67 episodes that have been distinguished and separated from each other by asterisks in the given version of *Būstān* (1396).

DOI: 10.4324/9781003371786-4

CHAPTER 1 OF *BŪSTĀN*

Table 3.1 Frequency of evidentials in the first chapter of *Būstān*

Chapter	Episodes with evidentials		Episodes without evidentials			
	Advice	Unknown source	Direct visual evidence	Heard	Quotation	Inferred/assumed
1 Number of cases	39	9	–	16	3	–
Occurrence frequency					63 direct, 4 indirect	

In 39 episodes **Sa'dī is advising** the reader. The specific cases in which advice is of pivotal concern will be as follows (note that the exact numbers in the original text have been listed):

خدا ترس را بر رعیت گمار
که معمار ملک است پرهیزگار

Appoint the God-fearing one over the peasant;
Because, the abstinent one is the architect of the country.

قدیمان خود را بیفزای قدر
که هرگز نیاید ز پرورده غدر

Advance the rank of thy own old friends;
Because, treachery never comes from the cherished one.

غریبی که پر فتنه باشد سرش
میازار و بیرون کن از کشورش

The foreigner, whose head is intent on strife; injure not;
but, expel him from the country.

عمل گر دهی مرد منعم شناس
که مفلس ندارد ز سلطان هراس

If thou dost give service (place and rank) recognize the beneficent man;
Because, the poor man has no fear of the king.

یکی را که کردی معزول ز جاه
چو چندی برآید ببخشش گناه

8. One whom thou didst dismiss from dignity;
   Forgive his crime, when some time elapses.

چو خواهی که نامت بود جاودان
مکن نام نیک بزرگان نهان

9. When thou dost wish that thy name may be eternal;
   Conceal not the good name of the great ones.

به سمع رضا مشنو ایذای کس
وگر گفته آید به غورش برس

10. With the ear of approval, listen not to a person's injury;
    But, if the speech comes probe its depth.

وزیری که چاه من آبش بریخت
به فرسنگ باید ز مکرش گریخت

13. The wazír, whose reputation my rank spilled;
    It is necessary to fly from his deceit to the distance of a league.

نه بر حکم شرع آب خوردن خطاست
وگر خون به فتوا بریزی رواست

14. Is it not a crime to drink water, without the order of the Law of Religion?
    But, if by decree of the judge, thou dost shed blood, it is lawful.

تنت زورمند است و لشگر گران
ولیکن در اقلیم دشمن مران

15. Thy body is powerful, and army great;
    But, into the country of the enemy (of the kings of Islám) urge it not.

نظر کن در احوال زندانیان
که ممکن بود بی گنه در میان

16. Look into the affairs of prisoners:
    It is possible that a guiltless one may be among them.

$$\text{بیندیش از آن طفلک بی پدر}$$
$$\text{وز آه دل دردمندش حذر}$$

17. Think of that poor child, without father;
    And be cautious of the sigh of his sorrowful heart.

$$\text{سپاهی که خوشدل نباشد ز شاه}$$
$$\text{ندارد حدود ولایت نگاه}$$

19. The soldier, who, on account of his king, is not happy at heart,
    Watches not the borders of the kingdom.

$$\text{چو شاید گرفتن به نرمی دیار}$$
$$\text{به پیکان خون از مشامی میار}$$

20. When it is possible to take the country with gentleness,
    In contest, bring not forth blood from a single pore of the body.

$$\text{چو با دشمنی باشدت دسترس}$$
$$\text{مرنجانش کاو را همین غصه بس}$$

21. When thou hast power over an enemy, Injure him not;
    because this (the power) is indeed sufficient sorrow to him.

$$\text{چنان خسب کاید فغانت به گوش}$$
$$\text{اگر دادخواهی برآرد خروش}$$

23. So sleep, that the lamentation may come to thy ear,
    If the crier for justice brings forth a shout.

$$\text{نخواهی که باشد دلت دردمند}$$
$$\text{دل دردمندان برآور ز بند}$$

25. Thou dost not wish, that thy heart may be sorrowful;
    Bring forth from fetters the heart of the sorrowing ones.

اگر خوش بخسبد ملک بر سریر
نپندارم آسوده خسبد فقیر

27. If the king on the throne sleep pleasantly,
    I think not the poor man sleeps at ease.

مها زورمندی مکن با کهان
که بر یک نمط می نماند جهان

31. Oh great one! exercise not violence on the humble;
    Because, the world remains not in one way.

تحمل کن ای ناتوان از قوی
که روزی تواناتر از وی شوی

32. Oh feeble one! endure (the tyranny) of the strong;
    Because, one day, thou mayst be stronger than he.

گرفتم کز افتادگان نیستی
چو افتاده بینی چرا نیستی؟

33. . . . I have granted that thou art not of (the number of) the fallen:
    When thou dost see a fallen one, why dost thou stand (and not give help)?

مگو جاهی از سلطنت بیش نیست
که ایمن تر از ملک درویش نیست

38. Say not—there is no dignity, higher than sovereignty;
    Because there is no empire safer than the empire of the darwesh.

نکوکار مردم نباشد بدش
نورزد کسی بد که نیک افتدش

40. The man of good work—evil is not to him:
    No one practices evil, that good may come to himself.

مزن بانگ بر شیرمردام درشت
چو با کودکان بر نیایی به مشت

43. Shout not against rough lion-like men,
    When with boys, in boxing, thou dost not prevail.

الا تا به غفلت نخفتی که نوم
حرام است بر چشم سالار قوم

44. Take care thou sleepst not in carelessness; because sleep;
    Is improper for the eyes of the leader of a tribe.

جهان ای پسر ملک جاوید نیست
ز دنیا وفاداری امید نیست

46. Oh Son! the world is not an everlasting country;
    There is no hope of the sincerity from the world.

همی تا بر آید به تدبیر کار
مدارای دشمن به از کارزار

55. So long as thy work prospers by deliberation,
    Courtesy to an enemy (is) better than contest.

بیندیش در قلب هیجا مفر
چه دانی که ز ان که باشد ظفر

56. Consider a place of retreat, in the heart of battle;
    Of that, what knowst thou,—that he may be conqueror?

دلاور که باری تهور نمود
بباید به مقدارش اندر فزود

57. The warrior, who has once showed ardour (in battle),
    It is proper to increase (his dignity), according to his worth.

به پیکار دشمن دلیران فرست
هژبران به ناورد شیران فرست

58. Send warriors to the contest with the enemy;
    Send lions to the conflict with lions.

یکی را که دیدی تو در جنگ پشت
بکش گر عدو در مصافش نکشت

59. The one, whose back thou seest in the day of battle, Slay,
if the enemy slay him not in the ranks.

دو تن پرور ای شاه کشور گشای
یکی اهل رزم و دگر اهل رای

60. Oh king, territory-conquering! cherish two persons;
One a man of arm (strong); the other, a man of judgment.

نگویم ز جنگ بد اندیش ترس
در آوازه صلح از او بیش ترس

61. I say not—fear battle with the enemy;
Fear rather him, who is in the state of peace.

میان دو بد خواه کوتاه دست
نه فرزانگی باشد ایمن نشست

62. Between two ill-wishers of short hand (weak),
It is not wisdom, to sit secure.

چو شمشیر پیکار برداشتی
نگه دار پنهان ره آشتی

63. When thou liftst up the sword of contest,
Look out, secretly, for the path of peace.

گرت خویش دشمن شود دوستدار
ز تلبیسش ایمن مشو زینهار

64. If a relation of the enemy be friendly to thee, Beware;
be not secure of craftiness.

سپاهی که عاصی شود در امیر
ورا تا توانی به خدمت مگیر

65. The soldier, who is an offender against the Amír,
So long as thou canst,—take not into service.

$$\text{چو اقلیم دشمن به جنگ و حصار}$$
$$\text{گرفتی، به زندانیانش سپار}$$

66. When, in battle and siege, the enemy's country,
Thou seizst,—consign it to the prisoners.

$$\text{به تدبیر جنگ بد اندیش کوش}$$
$$\text{مصالح بیندیش و نیت بپوش}$$

67. Essay with deliberation battle with the enemy;
Reflect on counsel; and, conceal thy resolution.

Episodes containing **no known source of evidentials** include instances that follow:

$$\text{ز دریای عمان برآمد کسی}$$
$$\text{سفر کرده هامون و دریا بسی}$$

11. A certain one came from the sea of 'Ummán,
Much sea and plain traveled;

$$\text{ندانم کجا دیده ام در کتاب}$$
$$\text{که ابلیس را دید شخصی به خواب}$$

12. I know not where in a book I have seen,
that a person in a dream saw Iblís.

$$\text{خبر یافت گردن کشی در عراق}$$
$$\text{که می گفت مسکینی از زیر طاق}$$

24. A certain neck-exalting one (a king), in Media, came to know
That a wretched one beneath an arch kept saying

$$\text{چنان قحط سالی شد اندر دمشق}$$
$$\text{که یاران فراموش کردند عشق}$$

34. Such a famine occurred in the city of Damascus,
    That lovers forgot love.

خبر داری از خسروان عجم
که کردند بر زیر دستان ستم

36. Thou hast knowledge of the Kings of Persia,
    Who exercised tyranny over their subjects?

گزیری به چاهی در افتاده بود
که از هول او شیر نر ماده بود

41. A man of war had fallen into a well
    Such a one that the male-tiger became female, from fear of him.

قزل ارسلان قلعه ای سخت داشت
که گردن به الوند بر می فراشت

48. King Kizil Arslán had a strong fort;
    That exalted its neck above the mountain Alwand.

چو آلپ ارسلان جان به جان بخش داد
پسر تاج شاهی به سر برنهاد

49. When Alap-Arslán gave his soul to the Soul-giver,
    The son placed the royal crown on his head.

چو دور خلافت به مامون رسید
یکی ماه پیکر کنیزک خرید

51. When the turn of the Khiláfat came to Mámún:
    He purchased a damsel with a face as the moon.

Episodes containing **heard evidentials** include numbers:

شنیدم که در وقت نزع روان
به هرمز چنین گفت نوشیروان

1. <u>I have heard</u> that, at the time of the agony of the soul (the last breath), (King) Naushíraván (the Just) thus spoke to Hurmuz (hisson),

شنیدم که خسرو به شیرویه گفت
در آن دم که چشمش ز دیدن بخفت

2. <u>I have heard</u> that King Khusrau said to (his son) Shírwiya
At that time when his eyes slept (rested) from seeing (at the time of death)

شنیدم که فرماندهی دادگر
قبا داشتی هر دو روی آستر

18. <u>I heard</u> that a just order-giver
Used to have a coat, both surfaces of lining (cheap) material.

شنیدم که دارای فرخ تبار
ز لشکر جدا ماند روز شکار

22. <u>I heard</u> that Darius of august family,
Became separated, on a hunting day, from his retinue

در اخبار شاهان پیشینه هست
که چون تکله بر تخت زنگی نشست

28. In the annals of former kings, it is written,
That when Tukla sat on the throne of Zangí.

شنیدم که بگریست سلطان روم
بر نیکمردی ز اهل علوم

29. <u>I heard</u> that the Sultán of Turkey wept,
Before a good man, possessed of sciences

خردمند مردی در اقصای شام
گرفت از جهان کنج غاری مقام

30. A wise man, in the boundaries of Syria, Took a cave, for his dwelling away from the world. . . . <u>I heard</u> that his name was—"Khudá-dost" (friend of God); He was of an angelic nature, man-in-form.

Evidentiality in Sa'dī's masterpieces

شبی دود خلق آتشی برفروخت
شنیدم که بغداد نیمی بسوخت

35. One night, the sigh of the people lighted up a fire.
    I heard that a half of the city of Baghdád was burned.

شنیدم که در مرزی از باختر
برادر دو بودند از یک پدر

37. I have heard that, in a territory of the west,
    There were two brothers (prince-sons), of one father (a king),

شنیدم که یک بار در حله ای
سخن گفت با عابدی کله ای

39. I once heard that, in a certain place,
    A skull spoke to an 'ábid,

حکایت کند از یکی نیکمرد
که اکرام حجاج یوسف نکرد

42. They relate a story of a certain good man,
    That he paid not respect to Hujjáj, the son of Joseph.

یکی را حکایت کند از ملوک
که بیماری رشته کردش چو دوک

45. They relate a story of one of the kings,
    Whom the disease of guinea-worm made like a spindle.

شنیدم که در مصر میری اجل
سپه تاخت بر روزگارش اجل

47. I have heard that, in respect to the glorious chief of Egypt,
    Death hastened an army on his life.

شنیدم که از پادشاهان غور
یکی پادشه خر گرفتی به زور

50. <u>I have heard</u> that of the monarchs of Ghúr,
    A certain king used to seize asses by force.

شنیدم که از نیکمردی فقیر
دل آزرده شد پادشاهی کبیر

52. <u>I have heard</u> that, on account of a good man, a fakír,
    The heart of a proud king became troubled.

یکی مشت زن بخت و روزی نداشت
نه اسباب شامش مهیا نه چاشت

53. A certain boxer had neither fortune nor victuals;
    The means ready—neither for his evening nor for his morning repast . . .

شنیدم که روزی زمین می شکافت
عظام زنخدان پوسیده یافت

<u>I heard</u> that he was, one day, breaking up the earth;
He found a rotten chin-bone.

Episodes containing **quoted source of evidentials** include numbers:

چه خوش گفت بازرگانی اسیر
چو گردش گرفتند دزدان به تیر

4. How well said the captive merchant
   When the robbers gathered around him with arrows!

مرا همچنان نام نیک است لیک
ز علت نگوید بد اندیش نیک

13. "Just so I (the new wazír) have a good name; but,
    "For reason, the evil-intent one speaks not good (of me) . . ."

ملک در سخن گفتنش خیره ماند
سر دست فرماندهی برفشاند

The king remained confounded at his speech:
He spread the tip of the hand of Order-Giving,

یکی از بزرگان اهل تمیز
حکایت کند ز ابن عبدالعزیز

26. One of the great ones, possessed of discretion,
Tells a story of the son of King 'Abdu-l-'Azíz.

In this chapter of the book there cannot be found any episode that is mainly based on the inferences or the assumptions of the author. Meanwhile, the total frequency of occurrence of direct speech as used in different parts of the whole chapter is much more than the application of indirect speech. The overall results show that letting alone the number of advices, the total number of indirect evidentials (19) is much more than episodes without known evidentials (9). Here, there cannot be found any story which is the result of direct visual experience.

The second chapter of *Būstān*, called "On Beneficence," contains 36 episodes separated from each other in the given version. Refer to Table 3.2.

CHAPTER 2 OF *BŪSTĀN*

Table 3.2 Frequency of evidentials in second chapter of *Būstān*

Chapter	Episodes without evidentials	Episodes with evidentials				
		Advice	Unknown source	Direct visual evidence	Heard	Quotation	Inferred/ assumed
2 Number of cases Occurrence frequency	9	14	2	11	68 direct, 12 indirect	–

In nine episodes Sa'dī **is advising** the reader which contains numbers:

اگر هوشمندی به معنی گرای
که معنی ز صورت بماند به جای

1. If thou art wise, incline to truth;
   For truth, not the semblance, remains in its place.

پدر مرده را سایه بر سر فکن
غبارش بیفشان و خارش بکن

2. Cast protection over the head of the one father-dead;
   Scatter his dust (of affliction), and pluck out his thorn

مشو تا توانی ز رحمت بری
که رحمت برندت چو رحمت بری

3. So long as thou canst, be not free from mercy;
   For they bear pity to thee, when thou bearst pity.

گره بر سر احسان بر مزن
که این زرق و شیدست و آن مکر و فن

5. Make not a knot at the head of the ligature of beneficence,
   Saying:—"This one is of fraud and deceit: and, that one of treachery and guile."

تو با خلق شاهی کن ای نیک بخت
که فردا خدا نگیرد با تو سخت

13. Oh one of happy fortune! do good to the people,
    That to-morrow, (the Judgment Day) God may not take hard (measures) with thee.

ببخش ای پسر کآدمی زاده صید
به احسان توان کرد و، وحشی به قید

16. Oh son! bestow; for, the one man-born, a prey,
    One can make by benefits; and, the wild beast, by restraint.

الا گر طلبکار اهل دلی
ز خدمت مکن یک زمان غافلی

27. Verily, if thou art a seeker of the pious one,
    Exercise not carelessness, a moment, as to his service.

در معرفت بر کسانی است باز
که درهاست بر روی ایشان فراز

30. The door of the knowledge of God is open to those,
    In whose face, the doors of men are shut.

بگفتیم در باب احسان بسی
ولیکن نه شرط است با هر کسی

34. As to beneficence, I said much;
    But, it is not proper for everyone.

Episodes containing **no known source of evidentials** include the following numbers:

زباندانی آمد به صاحبدلی
که محکم فرومانده ام در گلی

6. One, tongue-knowing, came to a pious man,
   Saying:—"I have stuck firmly in the mire."

یکی رفت و دینار از او صد هزار
خلف برد صاحبدلی هوشیار

7. One departed (from the world), and a hundred thousand
   dínars of his, The heir, a sensible pious man, took.

بزارید وقتی زنی پیش شوی
که دیگر مخر نان ز بقال کوی

8. Once upon a time, a wife lamented to her husband,
   Saying:—"Purchase not again bread from the general vendor of the street."

به سرهنگ سلطان چنین گفت زن
که خیز ای مبارک در رزق زن

10. A wife thus spoke (to her husband) an officer of the Sultán,
    Saying:—"Oh fortunate one! Arise; knock at the door of food."

یکی در بیابان سگی تشنه یافت
برون از رمق در حیاتش نیافت

12. A certain one found, in the desert, a thirsty dog;
    He found not beyond a spark of life in him.

بنالید درویشی از ضعف حال
بر تندرویی خداوند مال

14. A certain darvesh complained of weakness of state,
    To one of stern face, lord of wealth.

یکی سیرت نیکمردان شنو
اگر نیکبختی و مردانه رو

15. Hear a trait of good men,
    If thou art a good man, and of manly gait.

که شبلی ز حانوت گندم فروش
به ده برد انبان گندم به دوش

When Shiblí, from the shop of the wheat-seller,
Carried a wallet of wheat, on his back, to the village.

یکی روبهی دید بی دست و پای
فرو ماند در لطف و صنع خدای

18. A certain one saw a fox, legless and footless,
    He was astonied at the grace and creation of God.

چو حاتم به آزادمردی دگر
ز دوران گیتی نیامد مگر

24. Another in generosity, like Hátim,
    Comes not, perhaps, from the world's revolution.

یکی را خری در گل افتاده بود
ز سوداش خون در دل افتاده بود

25. Of a certain one, an ass had fallen into the mire;
    The blood, through phrenzy, had gathered to his heart.

Evidentiality in Sa'dī's masterpieces

یکی را پسر گم شد از راحله
شبانگه بگردید در قافله

28. The son of a certain one was lost from a camel-litter;
The father wandered about, in the night-time, in the káfila.

ز تاج ملکزاده ای در مناخ
شبی لعلی افتاد در سنگلاخ

29. From the crown of one king-born, in a camel-stable,
A ruby fell, one night, in a stony place.

یکی زهره خرج کردن نداشت
زرش بود و یارای خوردن نداشت

31. A certain one possessed not the power of spending;
Gold, he had; the power of enjoying, he had not.

جوانی به دانگی کرم کرده بود
تمنای پیری بر آورده بود

32. A young man had exercised liberality to the extent of a dáng; He had accomplished an old man's desire.

کسی دید صحرای محشر به خواب
مس تفته روی زمین ز آفتاب

33. In a dream, a person beheld the plain of the place of assembling:
The earth's surface, from sun,—molten copper.

Episodes containing **seen/visual evidentials** include the following numbers:

به ره بر یکی پیشم آمد جوان
به تک در پیش گوسفندی دوان

17. A young man came before me, on the road,
A sheep, running in bounds, behind him.

$$\text{من و چند سالوک صحرا نورد}$$
$$\text{برفتیم قاصد به دیدار مرد}$$

I and some other travellers, desert-wandering,
Went a-travelling for the sake of <u>seeing</u> the man.

Episodes containing **heard evidentials** include the following numbers:

$$\text{شنیدم که یک هفته ابن‌السبیل}$$
$$\text{نیامد به مهمانسرای خلیل}$$

4. I <u>have heard</u> that, one week, a son of the road (a traveller)
   Came not to the guest-house of (Ibráhím) the friend of God.

$$\text{شنیدم که پیری به راه حجاز}$$
$$\text{به هر خطوه کردی دو رکعت نماز}$$

9. I <u>have heard</u> that an old man, on the road to Hijáz,
   Used to make two prayer-motions, at every step.

$$\text{یکی را کرم بود و قوت نبود}$$
$$\text{کفافش به قدر مروت نبود}$$

11. To a certain one, liberality was; but power was not;
    Means of subsistence, to the extent of his generosity, were not.
    . . . . . .

$$\text{شنیدم که در حبس چندی بماند}$$
$$\text{نه شکوت نوشت و نه فریاد خواند}$$

<u>I heard that</u> he remained some time in prison;
He neither wrote to any one a complaint; nor, uttered a lament.

$$\text{شنیدم که مردی است پاکیزه بوم}$$
$$\text{شناسا و رهرو در اقصای روم}$$

19. I <u>have heard</u> that there was a man of pure birthplace,
    A recognizer, and road-traveller (in the way of God), in the confines of Rúm.

شنیدم در ایام حاتم که بود
به خیل اندرش بادپایی چو دود

20. I have heard that, in the time of Hátim, there was,
Among his horses, one swift footed, like smoke.

ندانم که گفت این حکایت به من
که بوده ست فرماندهی در یمن

21. I know not, who told me this tale,
That there had been, in the country of Yaman, an order-giver.

شنیدم که طی در زمان رسول
نکردند منشور ایمان قبول

22. I have heard that, in the time of the Prophet, the tribe of
Tai Made not acceptance of the faith (of the Kurán).

ز بنگاه حاتم یکی پیرمرد
طلب ده درم سنگ فانید کرد

23. From Hátim's store-house, an old man
Demanded ten diram's weight of sugar candy
. . . .

ز راوی چنان یاد دارم خبر
که پیشش فرستاد تنگی شکر

From the historian, I remember news such,
That he sent him a sack of sugar.

شنیدم که مغروری از کبر مست
در خانه بر روی سایل ببست

26. I have heard that a proud man, from pride-intoxication,
Shut the door of his house in a beggar's face.

شنیدم که مردی غم خانه خورد
که زنبور بر سقف او لانه کرد

35. <u>I have heard</u> that a man experienced house-vexation;
For, a wasp made a nest in his roof.

Meanwhile, some episodes contain 68 direct and 12 indirect speeches have been used. In this chapter of the book there cannot be found any episode that is mainly based on the inferences or the assumptions of the author. Meanwhile the total frequency of occurrence of direct speech as used in different parts of the whole chapter is much more than the application of indirect speech.

The third chapter of *Būstān*, called "On Love," contains 28 episodes separated from each other. Refer to Table 3.3.

CHAPTER 3 OF *BŪSTĀN*

Table 3.3 Frequency of evidentials in third chapter of *Būstān*

Chapter	Episodes without evidentials		Episodes with evidentials			
	Advice	Unknown source	Direct visual evidence	Heard	Quotation	Inferred/assumed
3 Number of cases	5	13	1	9	–	–
Occurrence frequency					51 direct, 1 indirect	

In five episodes **Sa'dī is advising the reader** which contains the following numbers:

خوشا وقت شوریدگان غمش
اگر زخم بینند و گر مرهمش

1. OH happy the time of those distraught in love of Him,
   Whether they experience the wound (of separation); or, the plaster (of propinquity to Him)!

تو را عشق همچون خودی ز آب و گل
رباید همی صبر و آرام دل

2. The love of one, like thyself—of water and clay,
   Ravishes patience and heart-ease.

چو عشقی که بنیاد آن بر هواست
چنین فتنه انگیز و فرمانرواست

3. When love, whose foundation is on desire,
   Is, to such a degree, tumult-exciting and command-issuing,

ره عقل جز پیچ بر پیچ نیست
بر عارفان جز خدا هیچ نیست

20. Wisdom's path is not, save turning on turning;
    Before holy men there is nothing, save God.

اگر مرد عشقی کم خویش گیر
و گر نه ره عافیت پیش گیر

25. If thou art a man of love, lose thyself;
    And, if not,—take the path of ease.

Episodes containing **no known source of evidentials** include the following numbers:

یکی شاهدی در سمرقند داشت
که گفتی به جای سمر قند داشت

7. A certain one had a mistress in Samarkand;
   Thou wouldst say: She possessed sugar, in place of speech.

یکی تشنه می گفت و جان می سپرد
خنک نیکبختی که در آب مرد

8. A certain one thirsty was saying, while he surrendered his
   soul:—"Happy is that fortunate one, who in water died!"

یکی در نشابور دانی چه گفت
چو فرزندش از فرض خفتن بخفت

11. You know what a certain one said in Neshabour
    While his son fall to sleep from sleep deprevation

شکایت کند نوعروسی جوان
به پیری ز داماد نامهربان

12. A new young bride complains,
    To an old man (her father), of her unkind husband.

میان دو عم زاده وصلت فتاد
دو خورشید سیمای مهتر نژاد

15. Between two uncle-born ones, marriage occurred:
    Two of sun-face, of high descent.

یکی پیش شوریده حالی نبشت
که دوزخ تمنا کنی یا بهشت

16. A certain one to one of distraught state, wrote,
    Saying:—"Desirest thou hell, or heaven?"

به مجنون کسی گفت کای نیک پی
چه بودت که دیگر نیایی به حی؟

17. A certain one spoke to Majnún, saying:—"Oh one of auspicious foot!
    "What happened to thee, that thou comest not again to Hayy?

یکی خرده بر شاه غزنین گرفت
که حسنی ندارد ایاز ای شگفت

18. A certain one took up reproach against Mahmúd of Ghaznín,
    Saying:—"Áyáz has no (great) beauty. Oh wonder.

رییس دهی با پسر در رهی
گذشتند بر قلب شاهنشهی

21. The chief of a village, with his son, on a certain road,
    Passed by the center of a monarch's army.

مگر دیده باشی که در باغ و راغ
بتابد به شب کرمکی چون چراغ

22. Perhaps, thou mayst have seen, in the garden or meadow,
    How the fire-fly gleams at night, lamp-like?

یکی گفتش ای کرمک شب فروز
چه بودت که بیرون نیایی به روز

One said to it:—"Oh fire-fly, night-illuminating!"
"What is the matter with thee, that thou comest not forth by day?"

یکی را چو من دل به دست کسی
گرو بود و می برد خواری بسی

24. Of a certain one like me, the heart to the power of a
    Person was pledged; and, he endured much contempt.

شکر لب جوانی نی آموختی
که دلها در آتش چو نی سوختی

26. A young man of sugar-lip used to blow the flute;
    In such a way, that he used to burn hearts in the fire, reed-like.

کسی گفت پروانه را کای حقیر
برو دوستی در خور خویش گیر

27. A person said to a moth:—"Oh contemptible one!"
    "Go; take a friend suitable to thyself."

Episodes containing **heard evidentials** include the following numbers:

شنیدم که وقتی گدازاده ای
نظر داشت با پادشازاده ای

4. I have heard that, once upon a time, one, beggar-born,
   Had affection for one, king-born.*

شنیدم که بر لحن خنیاگری
به رقص اندر آمد پری پیکری

5. <u>I have heard</u>, that at the chanting of a singer,
   One of Parí face began to dance.

چنین دارم از پیر داننده یاد
که شوریده ای سر به صحرا نهاد

6. <u>I recollect hearing</u> from a knowing old man, in this way,
   That one, distraught with love, turned his head to the desert.

چنین نقل دارم ز مردان راه
فقیران منعم گدایان شاه

9. <u>I have a tale</u> of this sort—of the men of the way of God,
   Rich mendicants; king beggars;

شنیدم که پیری شبی زنده داشت
سحر دست حاجت به حق بر فراشت

10. <u>I heard that</u> an old man kept awake the night;
    In the morning, he raised the hand of need to God.

طبیبی پری چهره در مرو بود
که در باغ دل قامتش سرو بود

13. In Marv, there was a physician of Parí cheek,
    Whose stature, in the garden of the heart, was a cypress.

حکایت کند دردمندی غریب
که خوش بود چندی سرم با طبیب

A sorrowful wanderer <u>relates a tale</u>,
Saying:—"Some time, I had love for the physician."

یکی پنجه آهنین راست کرد
که با شیر زورآوری خواست کرد

14. A certain one established (by training) an iron grasp,
    Who wished to grapple with the lion.

. . . .

شنیدم که مسکین در آن زیر گفت
نشاید بدین پنجه با شیر گفت

I heard that the wretch, beneath that (lion), said:—
"It is not possible with this grasp to battle with the lion."

به شهری در از شام غوغا فتاد
گرفتند پیری مبارک نهاد

23. In a city of Syria, tumult occurred;
They seized an old man of happy nature.

هنوز آن حدیثم به گوش اندر است
چو قیدش نهادند بر پای و دست

Within my ear, still is that speech,
—When they placed fetters on his feet and hands,—

شبی یاد دارم که چشمم نخفت
شنیدم که پروانه با شمع گفت

28. One night, I recollect that my eyes slept not;
I heard that a moth spoke to a candle,

Episodes containing **seen/visual evidentials** only includes episode number 19.

قضا را من و پیری از فاریاب
رسیدیم در خاک مغرب به آب

19. By chance I and an old man from Faryáb
Arrived at a water (of a river) in the soil of the West.

In this chapter of the book there cannot be found any episode that is mainly based on the inferences or the assumptions of the author. Meanwhile, the total frequency of occurrence of direct speech as used in different parts of the whole chapter is much more than the use of indirect speech.

    The fourth chapter of *Būstān*, called "On Humility," contains 29 episodes separated from each other (see Table 3.4).

CHAPTER 4 OF *BŪSTĀN*

Table 3.4 Frequency of evidentials in fourth chapter of *Būstān*

Chapter		Episodes without evidentials		Episodes with evidentials			
		Advice	Unknown source	Direct visual evidence	Heard	Quotation	Inferred/ assumed
4	Number of cases	3	14	–	12	–	–
	Occurrence frequency				58 direct, 3 indirect		

In three episodes **Sa'dī <u>is advising</u>** the reader which contains numbers:

ز خاک آفریدت خداوند پاک
پس ای بنده افتادگی کن چو خاک

1. The pure Lord created thee from dust,
   Then, oh slave, practice humility like dust.

یکی قطره باران ز ابری چکید
خجل شد چو پهنای دریا بدید

2. rain-drop dropped from a cloud;
   It became ashamed, when it beheld the amplitude of the ocean . . . .

بزرگان نکردند در خود نگاه
خدابینی از خویشتن بین مخواه

5. The great showed not regard to themselves;
   Desire not God-beholding from one self-beholding.

Episodes containing **no known source of evidentials** include the following numbers:

جوانی خردمند پاکیزه بوم
ز دریا بر آمد به دربند روم

3. A wise youth of pure disposition
   Came forth from the sea, at the barrier of Rúm.

فقیهی کهن جامه تنگدست
در ایوان قاضی به صف بر نشست

7. A certain lawyer of tattered garment, of straightened hand,
   Sat down in the foremost ranks, in the hall of the Kází.

یکی پادشه زاده در گنجه بود
که دور از تو ناپاک و سرپنجه بود

8. There was in the town of Ganja,—one king-born,
   Who was unclean and tyrannical—may it be far from thee!—

شکار خنده ای انگبین می فروخت
که دلها ز شیرینیش می بسوخت

9. One of sugar-laughter sold honey,
   From whose sweetness, hearts become consumed.

سگی پای صحرانشینی گزید
به خشمی که زهرش ز دندان چکید

11. The foot of one desert-sitting, a certain dog bit
    With such anger, that poison dropped from his teeth.

بزرگی هنرمند آفاق بود
غلامش نکوهیده اخلاق بود

12. There was a certain great one, skillful in the world;
    His slave was of depraved qualities.

طمع برد شوخی به صاحبدلی
نبود آن زمان در میان حاصلی

14. An impudent one preferred his desire (in beggary) to a pious one,
    There was not, at that time, a single acquired thing (money) in his girdle.

ملک صالح از پادشاهان شام
برون آمدی صبحدم با غلام

15. King Sálih of the kings of Syria
    Used to come out early in the morning with his slave.

یکی در نجوم اندکی دست داشت
ولی از تکبر سری مست داشت

16. A certain one had a little skill in astronomy;
    But, he possessed a head, intoxicated with pride.

ز ویرانه عارفی ژنده پوش
یکی را نباح سگ آمد به گوش

18. From the desolate place of a holy man, ragged garment clad,
    The baying of a dog came to a certain one's ear.

عزیزی در اقصای تبریز بود
که همواره بیدار و شب خیز بود

20. There was, in the limits of Tabríz, one dear to God,
    Who was always wakeful and night-rising (in devotion).

یکی را چو سعدی دلی ساده بود
که با ساده رویی در افتاده بود

21. There was a pure heart, Sa'dī-like, to a certain one,
    Who had fallen in love with one of smooth face.

یکی بربطی در بغل داشت مست
به شب در سر پارسایی شکست

24. A certain drunken one had a harp under his arm;
    He broke it, at night, on a devotee's head.

یکی خوب کردار خوش خوی بود
که بد سیرتان را نکو گوی بود

28. Of good conduct and good disposition, there was a certain one,
    Who was well-speaking of the bad.

Evidentiality in Sa'dī's masterpieces   57

Episodes containing **heard evidentials** include the following numbers:

شنیدم که روزی سحرگاه عید
ز گرمابه آمد برون بایزید

4. I have heard that, once upon a time, on the morning of
   an 'íd, Báyizid came out of the hot bath.

شنیدستم از راویان کلام
که در عهد عیسی علیه السلام

6. A compiler of the traditions, thus related, in talk,
   That, in the time of 'Ísa (on Him be peace!)

شنیدم که فرزانه ای حق پرست
گریبان گرفتش یکی رند مست

10. I have heard that of a learned man, God-worshipping,—
    His collar, a drunken knave seized.

کسی راه معروف کرخی بجست
که بنهاد معروفی از سر نخست

13. No one sought the road to the ancient shaikh Ma'rúf of Karkh,
    Who placed not, first, his own renown, out of his head.

شنیدم که مهمانش آمد یکی
ز بیماریش تا به مرگ اندکی

I heard that a certain one came a guest to him;
From his sickness to death little remained.

به خشم از ملک بنده ای سربتافت
بفرمود جستن کسش در نیافت

17. In anger, a slave turned his head from a king (fled);
    He ordered a person to seek; no one found him.
    . . . .

شنیدم که گفت از دل تنگ ریش
خدایا بحل کردمش خون خویش

I heard that, from his straightened heart, he said:—
"Oh God! I pardon him my blood,

گروهی برآنند از اهل سخن
که حاتم اصم بود، باور مکن

19. A number of the eloquent are of opinion, I heard
That Hátim was deaf; believe it not

شنیدم که لقمان سیه فام بود
نه تن پرور و نازک اندام بود

22. I have heard that Lukmán was of black color;
Was neither tender, as to body; nor, delicate, as to limb.

شنیدم که در دشت صنعا جنید
سگی دید برکنده دندان صید

23. I have heard that, in the desert of San'á, Juníd
Saw a dog (by old age) the hunting-teeth dug out.

شنیدم که در خاک وخش از مهان
یکی بود در کنج خلوت نهان

25. I heard that, in the dust of Wakhsh, of the great,
There was one hidden, in the corner of retirement.

کسی مشکلی برد پیش علی
مگر مشکلش را کند منجلی

26. A certain one brought a difficult matter before 'Alí;—
Per adventure, he may make apparent to him the difficulty.
. . . .

شنیدم که شخصی در آن انجمن
بگفتا چنین نیست یا بالحسن

I heard that, in this assembly, a person
Said:—"Oh Bú-l-Hasan! it is not so."

Evidentiality in Sa'dī's masterpieces

گدایی شنیدم که در تنگ جای
نهادش عمر پای بر پشت پای

27. I heard that, in a narrow street, as regards a beggar,
'Umar placed his own foot on the back of his foot.

چنین یاد دارم که سقای نیل
نکرد آب بر مصر سالی سبیل

29. I have recollection of this sort, that the water-carrier of the Nile
Prepared not, one year, water for Egypt.

. . . .

شنیدم که ذوالنون به مدین گریخت
بسی بر نیامد که باران بریخت

I heard that Zú-n-Nún fled to Madín;
Much time passed not before rain fell

In this chapter of the book there cannot be found any episode that is mainly based on the inferences or the assumptions of the author. Meanwhile the total frequency of occurrence of direct speech, as used in different parts of the whole chapter, is much more than the application of indirect speech.

The fifth chapter of *Būstān*, called "On Resignation," contains 17 episodes separated from each other (see Table 3.5).

CHAPTER 5 OF *BŪSTĀN*

Table 3.5 Frequency of evidentials in fifth chapter of *Būstān*

Chapter	Episodes without evidentials		Episodes with evidentials			
	Advice	Unknown source	Direct visual evidence	Heard	Quotation	Inferred/ assumed
5 Number of cases Occurrence frequency	2	6	2	4	3 21 direct, 1 indirect	—

In two episodes Sa'dī is advising the reader which contains the following numbers:

سعادت به بخشایش داورست
نه در چنگ و بازوی زور آورست

2. Happiness is in the gift of the Ruler (God);
   It is not in the grasp and arm of the strong.

عبادت به اخلاص نیت نکوست
وگر نه چه آید ز بی مغز پوست

14. Worship, with sincerity of intention, is good;
    Otherwise, what comes from the husk, without kernel?

Episodes containing **no known source of evidentials** include the following numbers:

شبی کردی از درد پهلو نخفت
طبیبی در آن ناحیت بود و گفت

shabi kordi az dard-e pahlu nakhoft
tabibi dar ān nāhiyat bud-o goft

5. One night, a hero slept not on account of a side-pain;
   There was a physician, in that quarter; he said:—

یکی روستایی سقط شد خرش
علم کرد بر تاک بستان سرش

6. As to a certain villager,—his ass fell (and died);
   On a vine-tendril, he placed its head flag-fashion.

فرو کوفت پیری پسر را به چوب
بگفت ای پدر بی گناهم مکوب

8. An old man struck his son with a stick;
   He said:—"Oh father! I am guiltless; strike not."

Evidentiality in Sa'dī's masterpieces

بلند اختری نام او بختیار
قوی دستگه بود و سرمایه دار

9. One of lofty star,—his name Bakht-yár,
   Was of great power, and possessed of capital.

یکی مرد درویش در خاک کیش
چه خوش گفت با همسر زشت خویش

10. In the dust of Kísh, a certain poor man,
    How well he said to his ugly partner (wife)

ندانی که بابای کوهی چه گفت
به مردی که ناموس را شب نخفت

15. Knowst thou not what the old man of the mountain said,
    To the man, who, for reputation, slept not at night?

Episodes containing **heard evidentials** include the following numbers:

یکی آهنین پنجه در اردبیل
همی بگذرانید پیلک ز پیل

4. In Ardabíl, a certain one of iron grasp
   Caused, continually, the double-headed arrow to pass through a spade.*
   . . . .

شنیدم که می گفت و خون می گریست
ندانی که روز اجل کس نزیست

I heard that he said, while he wept blood:—
"Knowst thou not that no one lives on the day of death?"

شنیدم که دیناری از مفلسی
بیفتاد و مسکین بجستش بسی

7. I have heard that, from an indigent person, a dínár
   Fell; and that the wretched one sought for it much.

شنیدم که نابالغی روزه داشت
به صد محنت آورد روزی به چاشت

16. I have heard that a certain one of immature age kept a fast,
   With a hundred difficulties, he accomplished one day up to the mid-day meal.

سیه‌کاری از نردبانی فتاد
شنیدم که هم در نفس جان بداد

17. One of black deeds fell from a ladder;
   I heard that, even in a breath, he gave his soul (to God).

Episodes containing **directly seen evidentials** include the following numbers:

شبی زیت فکرت همی سوختم
چراغ بلاغت می افروختم

1. One night, I kept burning the olive-oil of reflection;
   I lighted up the lamp of eloquence.

مرا در سپاهان یکی یار بود
که جنگاور و شوخ و عیار بود

3. In Sipahán, I had a certain friend,
   Who was warlike and fearless and shrewd.

Episodes containing **quoted source of evidentials** include the following numbers:

چنین گفت پیش زغن کرکسی
که نبود ز من دوربین تر کسی

11. A vulture to a kite thus spoke,
    Saying:—"There is no one more far-seeing than myself."

چه خوش گفت شاگرد منسوج باف
چو عنقا بر آورد و پیل و زراف

12. How well said the apprentice of the embroidery-weaver,
    When he pourtrayed 'Anká, and elephant, and giraffe:—

شتر بچه با مادر خویش گفت
بس از رفتن آخر زمانی بخفت

13. A young camel, to its mother, said:—
    "After travelling, at last, sleep awhile."

In this chapter of the book there cannot be found any episode that is mainly based on the inferences or the assumptions of the author. Meanwhile the total frequency of occurrence of direct speech, as used in different parts of the whole chapter, is much more than the application of indirect speech.

The sixth chapter of *Būstān*, called "On Contentment," contains 16 episodes separated from each other (see Table 3.6).

CHAPTER 6 OF *BŪSTĀN*

Table 3.6 Frequency of evidentials in sixth chapter of *Būstān*

Chapter	Episodes without evidentials		Episodes with evidentials			
	Advice	Unknown source	Direct visual evidence	Heard	Quotation	Inferred/ assumed
6 Number of cases Occurrence frequency	2	8	2	4	– 18 direct, 1 indirect	–

In two episodes Sa'dī is advising the reader which contains the following numbers:

خدا را ندانست و طاعت نکرد
که بر بخت و روزی قناعت نکرد

1. He knew not God and worshipped not,
   Who displayed not contentment with his fortune and daily food

کمال است در نفس مرد کریم
گرش زر نباشد چه نقصان و بیم

15. The perfection (of existence) is the breath (spirit) of a gentle man,
    If he have not gold,—what loss or fear?

    Episodes containing <u>no known source of evidentials</u> are:

یکی را تب آمد ز صاحبدلان
کسی گفت شکر بخواه از فلان

4. To one of the holy men, a fever came,
   A person said:—"Ask for sugar from such a one."

شکم صوفیی را زبون کرد و فرج
دو دینار بر هر دوان کرد خرج

6. The Sufi was degraded for belly(eating) and vagina(sex),
   And spent his two Dinars on them.

یکی نیشکر داشت بر طبقری
چپ و راست گردیده بر مشتری

7. A certain one had sugar-cane, on a small plate,—
   A wanderer, left and right, for a purchaser.

یکی را ز مردان روشن ضمیر
امیر ختن داد طاقی حریر

8. To one of the men of illumined mind,
   The Amír of Khután gave a piece of silk cloth

یکی نان خورش جز پیازی نداشت
چو دیگر کسان برگ و سازی نداشت

9. A certain one had no bread-food, save an onion;
   He had no resources and means, like others

یکی گربه در خانه زال بود
که برگشته ایام و بد حال بود

10. In an old woman's house, there was a certain cat,
    Which was of reversed fortune, and of bad state.

یکی طفل دندان برآورده بود
پدر سر به فکرت فرو برده بود

11. A certain child had cut its teeth,
    The father was head-lowered in reflection,

یکی سلطنت ران صاحب شکوه
فرو خواست رفت آفتابش به کوه

14. As to a certain one, empire-ruling, possessed of pomp,—
    His sun (life) desired to descend to the mountain (in death).

Episodes containing <u>heard evidentials</u> are:

یکی پر طمع پیش خوارزمشاه
شنیدم که شد بامدادی پگاه

3. A certain one, possessed of avarice, before King Khwárazm,
   —I heard—went early in the morning.

شنیدی که در روزگار قدیم
شدی سنگ در دست ابدال سیم

12. I heard that, in ancient times,
    A stone used, in the hands of the pious, to become silver.

شنیدم که صاحبدلی نیکمرد
یکی خانه بر قامت خویش کرد

13. I have heard that a pious one, a good man,
    Made a house conformable to his stature.

شنیدم ز پیران شیرین سخن
که بود اندر این شهر پیری کهن

16. From men of sweet discourse, I have heard,
    That, there was within the city (of Shíráz) a certain ancient old man;

Episodes containing <u>seen/visual source of evidentials</u> include numbers 2 and 5.

66 Evidentiality in Sa'dī's masterpieces

مرا حاجیی شانه عاج داد
که رحمت بر اخلاق حجاج باد

2. A Hájí gave me an ivory comb,
Saying:—"May the mercy of God be on the good qualities of pilgrims!"

چه آوردم از بصره دانی عجب
حدیثی که شیرین تر است از رطب

5. Knowst thou what wonderful thing I brought from Basra?
—A tale, which is sweeter than the green date.

تنی چند در خرقه راستان
گذشتیم بر طرف خرماستان

We—a few individuals in the religious garb of the true (Súfís)—
Passed by the side of a date-garden.

In this chapter of the book there cannot be found any episode that is mainly based on the inferences or the assumptions of the author. Meanwhile, the total frequency of occurrence of direct speech, as used in different parts of the whole chapter, is much more than the application of indirect speech.

CHAPTER 7 OF *BŪSTĀN*

The seventh chapter of *Būstān*, called "On Education," contains 34 episodes separated from each other (see Table 3.7).

Table 3.7 Frequency of evidentials in seventh chapter of *Būstān*

Chapter	Episodes without evidentials		Episodes with evidentials			
	Advice	Unknown source	Direct visual evidence	Heard	Quotation	Inferred/ assumed
7 Number of cases Occurrence frequency	9	6	4	5	10 46 direct, 0 indirect	—

In these episodes Sa'dī is advising the reader which contains the following numbers:

سخن در صلاح است و تدبیر و خوی
نه در اسب و میدان و چوگان و گوی

1. The language (of this chapter) is on integrity, and deliberation, and disposition;
   Not on the steed, and the battle-field, and the ball-game.

اگر پای در دامن آری چو کوه
سرت ز آسمان بگذرد در شکوه

2. If thou bringst thy feet, mountain-like, (firmly) beneath thy skirt,
   Thy head will pass beyond the sky in grandeur.

دو کس گرد دیدند و آشوب و جنگ
پراکنده نعلین و پرنده سنگ

8. Two persons beheld dust, and tumult, and conflict;
   Shoes scattered; stones flying.

. . . .

کسی خوشتر از خویشتن دار نیست
که با خوب و زشت کسش کار نیست

No one is happier than one lord of himself;
For, he has no concern with the good and bad.

بد اندر حق مردم نیک و بد
مگوی ای جوانمرد صاحب خرد

11. In respect to the man, good or bad,—ill
    Utter not. Oh young man endowed with understanding!

کسی را که نام آمد اندر میان
به نیکوترین نام و نعتش بخوان

زن خوب فرمانبر پارسا
کند مرد درویش را پادشا

18. The person, whose name is mentioned in public,
    Recite his name and praises, in the sweetest way.

25. A good, order-bearing, chaste wife
    Makes a poor man, a king.

پسر چون ز ده بر گذشتش سنین
ز نامحرمان گو فراتر نشین

27. When a boy has passed ten years of age,
    Say:—"Sit apart from those not unlawful (to him in marriage)."

خرابت کند شاهد خانه کن
برو خانه آباد گردان به زن

29. The beardless boy, house-mining, ruins thee;
    Go; make the house prosperous with a pleasant woman.

اگر در جهان از جهان رسته ای است
در از خلق بر خویشتن بسته ای است

33. If he has escaped in the world, from the (people of the) world,
    It is he, who has closed the door on himself, against the people.

Episodes containing <u>no known source of evidentials</u> include the following numbers:

یکی خوب خلق خلق پوش بود
که در مصر یک چند خاموش بود

4. A certain one was of good disposition, but ragged garment clad,
   Who was silent for some time, in Egypt.

یکی ناسزا گفت در وقت جنگ
گریبان دریدند وی را به چنگ

Evidentiality in Sa'dī's masterpieces 69

5. A certain foolish one spoke at the time of quarrelling;
   With the hand, they rent his collar.

عضد را پسر سخت رنجور بود
شکیب از نهاد پدر دور بود

6. The son of King 'Azúd was very ill;
   Patience was far from his father's nature.

طریقت شناسان ثابت قدم
به خلوت نشستند چندی به هم

19. Those path-recognizing of firm foot
    Sat, some time, together in privacy.

فریدون وزیری پسندیده داشت
که روشن دل و دوربین دیده داشت

24. Fírídún had an approved vazír,
    Who possessed an illumined heart, and far-seeing eye.

یکی صورتی دید صاحب جمال
بگردیدش از شورش عشق حال

32. A certain (chaste) one saw a form possessed of beauty;
    Through phrensy of love and ecstacy for her, he changed.

Episodes containing <u>seen evidentials</u> include the following numbers:

مرا در نظامیه ادرار بود
شب و روز تلقین و تکرار بود

14. In the Nizámiya, I had a pension;
    Night and day, there was instruction and repetition.

به طفلی درم رغبت روزه خاست
ندانستمی چپ کدام است و راست

شبی دعوتی بود در کوی من
ز هر جنس مردم در او انجمن

28. One night, in my street, there was a convivial meeting;
    Men of every class, in that assembly.

جوانی هنرمند فرزانه بود
که در وعظ چالاک و مردانه بود

34. There was a young man, skillful and learned,
    Who was, as regards admonishing, vigilant and manly.
    . . . .

یکی را بگفتم ز صاحبدلان
که دندان پیشین ندارد فلان

I spoke to one of the pious,
Saying:—"A certain one has no front teeth."

Episodes containing <u>heard evidentials</u> include the following numbers:

شنیدم که در بزم ترکان مست
مریدی دف و چنگ مطرب شکست

7. I have heard that, at a banquet of intoxicated slaves,
   A disciple broke the minstrel's tambourine and harp.

شنیدم که از پارسایان یکی
به طیبت بخندید با کودکی

16. I have heard that one of the pious
    Laughed, jestingly, at a boy.

سه کس را شنیدم که غیبت رواست
وز این درگذشتی چهارم خطاست

21. As to three persons, I have heard that slander is lawful;
    When thou exceedst this, the fourth is a sin.

شنیدم که دزدی درآمد ز دشت
به دروازه سیستان برگذشت

22. I have heard that a thief entered from the desert,
    He passed by the gate of Sístán.

در این شهر باری به سمعم رسید
که بازرگانی غلامی خرید

30. Once upon a time, it reached my ear in this city (of Shíráz),
    That a certain merchant purchased a slave.

Episodes containing <u>quoted source of evidentials</u> include the following numbers:

تکش با غلامان یکی راز گفت
که این را نباید به کس باز گفت

3. Takash uttered a secret to his slaves,
   Saying:—"It is improper to unfold this secret to anyone."

چنین گفت پیری پسندیده هوش
خوش آید سخنهای پیران به گوش

9. Thus spoke an old man of approved sense,
   —The words of old men are pleasing to the ear.—

یکی پیش داود طائی نشست
که دیدم فلان صوفی افتاده مست

10. A certain one sat before Dá'ud of the tribe of Tai,
    Saying:—"I saw a certain Súfí fallen drunk."

زبان کرد شخصی به غیبت دراز
بدو گفت داننده ای سرفراز

12. A person made long his tongue, in slander;
    A sagacious one, head-exalting spoke to him,

کسی گفت و پنداشتم طیبت است
که دزدی بسامان تر از غیبت است

13. A person said—I thought it was a jest—
    "Thieving is more upright than slandering."

کسی گفت حجاج خون‌خوار‌ه‌ای است
دلش همچو سنگ سیه پاره‌ای است

15. A certain one said:—"Hujjáj is a blood-devourer,
    "His heart is like a piece of black stone.

چه خوش گفت دیوانه مرغزی
حدیثی کز او لب به دندان گزی

20. How well a distraught one of Margház uttered
    A saying, from the subtlety of which thou mayst bite the lip with the teeth:—

یکی گفت با صوفیی در صفا
ندانی فلانت چه گفت از قفا

23. A certain one said to a Súfí, possessed of purity;—
    "Knowst thou not what a certain person said behind thy back?"

جوانی ز ناسازگاری جفت
بر پیرمردی بنالید و گفت

26. A young man, from want of concordance with his wife,
    Bewailed to an old man, and said:—

گروهی نشینند با خوش پسر
که ما پاکبازیم و صاحب نظر

31. A crowd sat with a pleasant youth,
    Saying:—"We are honourable lovers, and possessed of discernment."

Evidentiality in Sa'dī's masterpieces 73

In this chapter of the book there cannot be found any episode that is mainly based on the inferences or the assumptions of the author. Meanwhile, the total frequency of occurrence of direct speech, as used in different parts of the whole chapter, is much more than the application of indirect speech. Refer to Table 3.8.

CHAPTER 8 OF *BŪSTĀN*

Table 3.8 Frequency of evidentials in eighth chapter of *Būstān*

Chapter	Episodes without evidentials		Episodes with evidentials			
	Advice	Unknown source	Direct visual evidence	Heard	Quotation	Inferred/ assumed
8 Number of cases	6	7	1	2	–	–
occurrence frequency				16 direct, 0 indirect		

In six episodes Sa'dī is advising the reader which contains the following numbers:

نفس می‌نیارم زد از شکر دوست
که شکری ندانم که در خورد اوست

1. I CANNOT express a breath for thanks to my Friend (God);
   For, I know not a word of praise that is worthy of Him.

ببین تا یک انگشت از چند بند
به صنع الهی به هم در فگند

3. Behold one finger, with how many joints,
   God, by creating, cast together.

شب از بهر آسایش توست و روز
مه روشن و مهر گیتی فروز

6. For the sake of thy ease, the night and day are;
   The resplendent moon and the sun, world-illuminating.

نداند کسی قدر روز خوشی
مگر روزی افتد به سختی کشی

7. A person knows not the value of a day of pleasure,
   Save on that day when he falls to hardship-enduring.

سرشته است باری شفا در عسل
نه چندان که زور آورد با اجل

14. God has created the power of convalescence in honey,
    Not to such an extent that it exercises power over death.

نخست او ارادت به دل در نهاد
پس این بنده بر آستان سر نهاد

15. First, He placed in thy heart desire of worship,
    Then His slave placed his head (in devotion) at His threshold.

Some episodes containing <u>no known source</u> of evidentials include the following numbers:

جوانی سر از رای مادر بتافت
دل دردمندش به آذر بتافت

2. A young man turned his head from his mother's judgment,
   Her sorrowful heart burned like fire.

ملک زاده ای ز اسب ادهم فتاد
به گردن درش مهره بر هم فتاد

4. One king-born fell from a black horse;
   A joint in his neck became dislocated.

یکی را عسس دست بر بسته بود
همه شب پریشان و دلخسته بود

9. The night-guard had bound a certain one's hand;
   He was, all night, afflicted, and heart-broken.

Evidentiality in Sa'dī's masterpieces 75

برهنه تنی یک درم وام کرد
تن خویش را کسوتی خام کرد

10. One of naked body made loan of one diram;
    He made for his body a garment of raw hide.

یکی کرد بر پارسایی گذر
به صورت جهود آمدش در نظر

11. A certain one passed by a holy man,
    He came to his sight, in the form of a Jew.

ز ره باز پس مانده‌ای می‌گریست
که مسکین تر از من در این دشت کیست؟

12. One left behind on the road was weeping,
    Saying:—"Than I in this desert, who is more wretched?"

فقیهی بر افتاده مستی گذشت
به مستوری خویش مغرور گشت

13. A lawyer passed by one fallen drunk;
    He became proud of his own abstinence.

Episodes containing <u>seen evidentials</u> include the following number:

بتی دیدم از عاج در سومنات
مرصع چو در جاهلیت منات

16. I beheld an idol of ivory in the (idol-temple) Somnáth,
    Gemmed like the (idol) Manát, in (the days of) ignorance.

Episodes containing <u>heard evidentials</u> include the following numbers:

شنیدم که پیری پسر را به خشم
ملامت همی کرد کای شوخ چشم

5. A certain one severely rubbed a boy's ears (chastised him),
   Saying:—"Oh father of wonderful judgment, of overturned fortune!

شنیدم که طغرل شبی در خزان
گذر کرد بر هندوی پاسبان

8. I have heard that Tughril, one night, in the autumn,
   Passed a Hindú watchman,

In this chapter of the book there cannot be found any episode that is mainly based on the inferences or the assumptions of the author. Meanwhile, the total frequency of occurrence of direct speech, as used in different parts of the whole chapter, is much more than the application of indirect speech.

CHAPTER 9 OF *BŪSTĀN*

Chapter 9 of *Būstān*, called "On Repentance," contains 23 episodes separated from each other (see Table 3.9).

Table 3.9 Frequency of evidentials in ninth chapter of *Būstān*

Chapter	Episodes without evidentials		Episodes with evidentials			
	Advice	Unknown source	Direct visual evidence	Heard	Quotation	Inferred/ assumed
9 Number of cases Occurrence frequency	4	11	8	–	25 direct, 1 indirect	–

In four episodes Sa'dī is advising the reader which contains numbers:

بیا ای که عمرت به هفتاد رفت
مگر خفته بودی که بر باد رفت

1. OH, thou whose age has passed to seventy years! Come;
   Thou wast, perhaps, asleep that thy life went to the wind.

جوانا ره طاعت امروز گیر
که فردا جوانی نیاید ز پیر

4. Oh young man; to-day (in youth), take the path of salvation;
   For, to-morrow, youth comes not from old age.

خبر داری ای استخوانی قفس
که جان تو مرغی است نامش نفس

11. Oh bone-cage! knowst thou
    That thy soul is a bird; and its name, spirit?

پلیدی کند گربه بر جای پاک
چو زشتش نماید بپوشد به خاک

20. The cat makes pollution, in a pure place;
    When it appears filthy, he covers it with dust.

Eleven episodes containing no known source of evidentials include the following numbers:

قضا زنده ای را رگ جان برید
دگر کس به مرگش گریبان درید

6. Fate cut the vein of Life of one living;
   Another, through grief, rent his collar.

فرو رفت جم را یکی نازنین
کفن کرد چون کرمش ابریشمین

7. A certain delicate one (a son) of (King) Jamshíd descended (to the grave),
   A shroud of silk, he made him, like the silk-worm.

یکی پارسا سیرت حق پرست
فتادش یکی خشت زرین به دست

8. As to one of devotee-disposition, God-worshipping,—
   A golden brick fell to his hand.

میان دو تن دشمنی بود و جنگ
سر از کبر بر یکدیگر چون پلنگ

9. Between two persons, there was enmity and strife,
   Through pride, head above the other, panther-like.

یکی برد با پادشاهی ستیز
به دشمن سپردش که خونش بریز

13. A certain one used contention with a king;
    He consigned him to his enemy, saying:—"Spill his blood."

یکی مال مردم به تلبیس خورد
چو برخاست لعنت بر ابلیس کرد

14. A certain one, by fraud, enjoyed a man's property.
    When it arose (and departed), he cursed Iblís.

گل آلوده ای راه مسجد گرفت
ز بخت نگون بود اندر شگفت

15. One clay-stained took the path to a masjid;
    From fortune of reversed fortune, in astonishment.

یکی غله مرداد مه توده کرد
ز تیمار دی خاطر آسوده کرد

17. A certain one heaped up the corn of the autumn month Mardad;
    He set his heart at ease, as to the care of the spring month Dai.*

یکی متفق بود بر منکری
گذر کرد بر وی نکو محضری

18. A certain one was consenting to a forbidden deed;
    One of good qualities passed by him.

زلیخا چو گشت از می عشق مست
به دامان یوسف در آویخت دست

19. When Zulaikhá became intoxicated with the wine of love,
    She fixed her hand on the skirt of Yúsuf.

یکی را به چوگان مه دامغان
بزد تا چو طبلش بر آمد فغان

22. The King of Damighán, with a chaugán, a certain one,
    Struck, so that his cry, drum-like, came forth.

Episodes containing <u>seen evidentials</u> include the following numbers:

شبی در جوانی و طیب نعم
جوانان نشستیم چندی بهم

2. One night, in youth and the pleasure of affluence (of youth), We, young men, sat sometime together.

کهنسالی آمد به نزد طبیب
ز نالیدنش تا به مردن قریب

3. One of ancient years <u>came</u> to a physician,
   From his weeping, near to dying,

شبی خوابم اندر بیابان فید
فرو بست پای دویدن به قید

5. One night, in the desert of Faid, sleep
   Bound down my foot of running with fetters.

شبی خفته بودم به عزم سفر
پی کاروانی گرفتم سحر

10. One night, I had slept with the intention of making a journey;
    In the morning, I followed a káravan.

ز عهد پدر یادم آید همی
که باران رحمت بر او هر دمی

12. I remember, in my father's time,
    —The rain of mercy, every moment on him!—

ز عهد پدر یادم آید همی
که باران رحمت بر او هر دمی

16. Recollection keeps coming to me of the time of childhood,
    When, on an 'Íd, I came out with my father.

غریب آمدم در سواد حبش
دل از دهر فارغ سر از عیش خوش

21. I came a traveller into a city of Abyssinia;
    Heart, from care, free; head, through ease, happy.

به صنعا درم طفلی اندر گذشت
چه گویم کز آنم چه بر سر گذشت

23. In Sin'á, a child of mine passed away (in death);
    Of that which passed over my head,—what may I say?*

In this chapter of the book there cannot be found any episode that is mainly based on the inferences or the assumptions of the author. Meanwhile, the total frequency of occurrence of direct speech, as used in different parts of the whole chapter, is much more than the application of indirect speech.

The last chapter of *Būstān*, called "On Prayer," contains five episodes separated from each other (see Table 3.10).

CHAPTER 10 OF *BŪSTĀN*

Table 3.10 Frequency of evidentials in tenth chapter of *Būstān*

Chapter	Episodes without evidentials		Episodes with evidentials				
	Advice	Unknown source	Direct visual evidence	Heard	Quotation	Inferred/assumed
10 Number of cases Occurrence frequency	1	3	–	1	– 6 direct, 0 indirect	–

In one episode Sa'dī is advising the reader which contains number 1.

بیا تا برآریم دستی ز دل
که نتوان برآورد فردا ز گل

1. COME; let us raise a hand from the heart;
   For, to-morrow, (after death), one cannot raise the hand from the clay (of the grave).

Episodes containing no known source of evidentials include numbers 2, 3, 4.

سیه چرده ای را کسی زشت خواند
جوابی بگفتش که حیران بماند

2. A certain one called one of blackish color, ugly;
   He gave to him an answer of such a sort that he remained astonied.

چه خوش گفت درویش کوتاه دست
که شب توبه کرد و سحرگه شکست

3. How well said the darvesh of short hand,
   Who, in the night, vowed; and, in the morning, broke his vow:—

مغی در به روی از جهان بسته بود
بتی را به خدمت میان بسته بود

4. An idolater was door shut as to his face against the world;
   He was loin-girt in an idol's service.

Episodes containing heard evidentials include number 5.

شنیدم که مستی ز تاب نبید
به مقصوره مسجدی در دوید

5. I have heard that one intoxicated with the heat of the date-wine,
   Ran to the most sacred place of a masjid.

In this chapter of the book there cannot be found any episode that is mainly based on the inferences or the assumptions of the author. Meanwhile, the total frequency of occurrence of direct speech, as used in different parts of the whole chapter, is much more than the application of indirect speech.

82 *Evidentiality in Sa'dī's masterpieces*

SUMMARY AND CONCLUSIONS

The overall results of the analysis show some facts about *Būstān* (see Tables 3.11 and 3.12).

Table 3.11 The overall results of evidentiality frequency in *Būstān*

Chapter	Episodes without evidentials		Episodes with evidentials			
	Advice	Unknown source	Direct visual evidence	Heard	Quotation	Inferred/assumed
Total number	80	91	20	64	423 direct 23 indirect	–

Table 3.12 Frequency of evidentials in *Būstān*

Chapters		Episodes without evidentials		Episodes with evidentials			
		Advice	Unknown source	Direct visual evidence	Heard	Quotation	Inferred/assumed
1	Number of cases Occurrence frequency	39	9	–	16	3 63 direct, 4 indirect	–
2	Number of cases Occurrence frequency	9	14	2	11	– 68 direct, 12 indirect	–
3	Number of cases Occurrence frequency	5	13	1	9	– 51 direct, 1 indirect	–
4	Number of cases Occurrence frequency	3	14	–	12	– 58 direct, 3 indirect	–
5	Number of cases Occurrence frequency	2	6	2	4	3 21 direct, 1 indirect	–
6	Number of cases Occurrence frequency	2	8	2	4	– 18 direct 1 indirect	–
7	Number of cases Occurrence frequency	9	6	4	5	10 46 direct, 0 indirect	–

Evidentiality in Sa'dī's masterpieces   83

Chapters	Episodes without evidentials		Episodes with evidentials				
	Advice	Unknown source	Direct visual evidence	Heard	Quotation	Inferred/ assumed	

8 Number of cases
   Occurrence
   frequency
	6	7	1	2	–
					16 direct,
					0 indirect
						–

9 Number of cases
   Occurrence
   frequency
	4	11	8	-	–
					25 direct,
					1 indirect
						–

10 Number of cases
   Occurrence
   frequency
	1	3	–	1	–
					6 direct,
					0 indirect
						–

Total number	80	91	20	64	423 direct 23 indirect	

1. Ignoring the number of poetic episodes in which Sa'dī is giving advices to the readers, the total number of episodes without known and specific evidentials is much more than the ones bearing any kind of evidentials so that in most narratives the narrator doesn't give us a hint or clue oh the source of information.
2. Second hand heard evidentials (represented by the word "Shenidam": I heard, in the book) are used more than the first hand visual evidentials showing that Sa'dī has heard more than seen the events and themes of the stories and narration.
3. The total number of direct speech as a kind of indirect evidentials is much more than indirect one. The function of this direct mechanism of speech can be considered as a compensatory means for the overuse of narratives which lack specific and known evidentials.
4. The total number of poetic episodes quoted from specific narrator is much less than the ones narrated from unknown sources. It shows that the author's tendency is to use unspecified sources for his narration.

3.2 *Golestān (Sa'dī, 1396b) translated by F. Gladwin (1865)*

FREQUENCY OF EVIDENTIALS IN *GOLESTĀN*

Tables illustrated in this section will show the frequency of occurrence of direct and indirect evidentials as has been used in *Golestān*.

CHAPTER 1 OF *GOLESTĀN*

The first chapter of *Golestān* on the morals of kings contains 41 stories (see Table 3.13).

Table 3.13 Frequency of evidentials in first chapter of *Golestān*

Chapter	Episodes without evidentials		Episodes with evidentials			
	Advice	Unknown source	Direct visual evidence	Heard	Quotation	Inferred/ assumed
1 Number of cases	–	21	6	9	5	–

In some stories of this chapter you will see that there is **no known evidential**, meaning the reader won't know how Sa'dī exactly knows the story and what his source of information is. These stories includes numbers

٢. یکی از ملوک خراسان محمود سبکتگین را به خواب چنان دید که جمله وجود او ریخته بود و خاک شده مگر چشمان او که همچنان در چشم خانه همی‌گردید و نظر می‌کرد.

2. ONE of the kings of Khorasan saw in a dream Sultan Mahmood Sebuktegeen a hundred years after his death, when the whole of his body had fallen into pieces and become dust, excepting his eyes, which moved in the sockets, and looked about ... TALE II. p. 113.

٤. طایفه دزدان عرب بر سر کوهی نشسته بودند و منفذ کاروان بسته و رعیت بلدان از مکاید ایشان مرعوب و لشکر سلطان مغلوب به حکم آنکه ملاذی منیع از قلّه کوهی گرفته بودند و ملجأ و مأوای خود ساخته.

4. A GANG of Arabian robbers had assembled on the top of a mountain, and blocked up the road of the caravan ... TALE IV. p. 116.

٧. پادشاهی با غلامی عجمی در کشتی نشست و غلام، دیگر دریا را ندیده بود و محنت کشتی نیازموده گریه و زاری در نهاد و لرزه بر اندامش اوفتاد.

7. A KING was sitting in a vessel with a Persian slave... TALE VII. p. 124.

۹. یکی از ملوک عرب رنجور بود در حالت پیری و امید زندگانی قطع کرده...

9. A KING of Arabia was sick in his old age, and there was no hope of his recovery,... TALE IX. p. 126.

۱۱. درویشی مستجاب الدعوه در بغداد پدید آمد حجاج یوسف را خبر کردند بخواندش و گفت دعای خیری بر من کن.

11. A DURWAISH, who never prayed in vain, made his appearance at Baghdad. Hojaj Yousuf sent for him, and said, "Offer up aprayer for me."... TALE XI. p. 128.

۱۵. یکی از وزرا معزول شد و به حلقه درویشان درآمد اثر برکت صحبت ایشان در او سرایت کرد و جمعیت خاطرش دست داد ملک بار دیگر بر او دل خوش کرد و عمل فرمود قبولش نیامد و گفت معزولی به نزد خردمندان بهتر که مشغولی.

15. A CERTAIN vizier, being dismissed from his office, joined a society of Durwaishes, the blessing of whose company made such an impression as bestowed comfort on his mind... TALE XV. p. 133.

۱۸. ملک زاده‌ای گنج فراوان از پدر میراث یافت. دست کرم بر گشاد و داد سخاوت بداد و نعمت بی دریغ بر سپاه و رعیت بریخت.

18. A PRINCE inherited from his father abundance of wealth... TALE XVIII. p. 141.

۲۲. یکی را از ملوک مرضی هایل بود که اعادت ذکر آن ناکردن اولی. طایفۀ حکمای یونان متفق شدند که مر این درد را دوایی نیست مگر زهره آدمی به چندین صفت موصوف. بفرمود طلب کردن.

22. A CERTAIN king had a terrible disease, the nature of which it is not proper to mention... TALE XXII. p. 146.

۲۳. یکی از بندگان عمرو لیث گریخته بود. کسان در عقبش برفتند و باز آوردند. وزیر را با وی غرضی بود و اشارت به کشتن فرمود تا دگر بندگان چنین فعل روا ندارند.

23. ONE of the slaves of Umroola is having absconded, a person was sent in pursuit of him, and brought him back... TALE XXIII. p. 148.

۲٤. ملک زوزن را خواجه‌ای بود کریم النفس نیک محضر که همگان را در مواجهه خدمت کردی و در غیبت نکویی گفتی.

24. A KING of Zuzan had a minister of a beneficent spirit and amiable disposition, who treated all persons with civility when present, and spoke well of them when absent... TALE XXIV. p. 149.

۲۵. یکی از ملوک عرب شنیدم که متعلقان را همی‌گفت مرسوم فلان را چندان که هست مضاعف کنید که ملازم درگاه است و مترصد فرمان و دیگر خدمتکاران به لهو و لعب مشغول‌اند و در ادای خدمت متهاون.

25. A KING of Arabia commanded his ministers to double the stipend of some one, because he was constant in his attendance, and always attentive to his duty, whilst the rest of the courtiers were dissipated in their manners and negligent of their business... TALE XXV. p. 152.

۲۷. یکی در صنعت کشتی گرفتن سرآمده بود، سیصد و شصت بند فاخر بدانستی و هر روز به نوعی از آن کشتی گرفتی.

27. A PERSON had arrived at the head of his profession in the art of wrestling; he knew three hundred and sixty capital sleights in this art, and every day exhibited something new;... TALE XXVII. p. 154.

۲۸. درویشی مجرد به گوشه‌ای نشسته بود. پادشاهی بر او بگذشت. درویش از آنجا که فراغ ملک قناعت است سر بر نیاورد و التفات نکرد.

28. A SOLITARY Durwaish had taken up his abode in a corner of a desert ... TALE XXVIII. p. 156.

۳۰. پادشاهی به کشتن بیگناهی فرمان داد. گفت: ای ملک به موجب خشمی که تو را بر من است آزار خود مجوی که این عقوبت بر من به یک نفس به سر آید و بزه آن بر تو جاوید بماند.

30. A KING having commanded an innocent person to be put to death, he said, "O king, seek not your own injury by venting your wrath on me." The king asked, in what manner... TALE XXX. p. 158.

۳۱. وزرای نوشیروان در مهمّی از مصالح مملکت اندیشه همی‌کردند و هر یکی از ایشان دگرگونه رای همی‌زدند و ملک همچنین تدبیری اندیشه کرد.

31. THE ministers of Nowshirvan were consulting on state affairs of great importance, and every one gave his opinion according to the best of his judgment: the king, in like manner, delivered his sentiments... TALE XXXI. p. 158.

۳۲. شیّادی گیسوان بافت که من علویم و با قافله حجاز به شهری در آمد که از حج همی‌آیم و قصیده‌ای پیش ملک برد که من گفته‌ام.

32. A CERTAIN impostor who had twisted his ringlets, pretending to be a descendant of Ah, entering the city, along with the caravan from Hejaz, said he was a pilgrim from Mecca, and presented the king with an elegy, as his own composition... TALE XXXII. p. 159.

۳٤. یکی از پسران هارون الرشید پیش پدر آمد خشم آلود که فلان سرهنگ زاده مرا دشنام مادر داد.

34. ONE of the sons of Haroon ur Rusheed went to his father in a rage, complaining that the son of a certain officer had spoken disrespectfully of his mother... TALE XXXIV. p. 161.

۳٦. دو برادر یکی خدمت سلطان کردی و دیگر به زور بازو نان خوردی.

36. THERE were two brothers, one of whom was in the service of the king, and the other ate the bread of his own industry... TALE XXXVI. p. 163.

۳۷. کسی مژده پیش انوشیروان عادل آورد، گفت: شنیدم که فلان دشمن تو را خدای عزّ و جلّ برداشت.

37. SOMEBODY brought to Noushirvan the Just the good tidings, that the God of majesty and glory has taken away such an one, who was your enemy... TALE XXXVII. p. 164.

۳۸. گروهی حکما به حضرت کسری در به مصلحتی سخن همی‌گفتند و بزرگمهر که مهتر ایشان بود خاموش.

38. AT the court of Kisra a number of wise men were debating on some affair, when, Buzerchemeher being silent, they asked him why in this debate he did not say anything... TALE XXXVIII. p. 164.

۴۰. یکی را از ملوک کنیزکی چینی آوردند. خواست تا در حالت مستی با وی جمع آید کنیزک ممانعت کرد. ملک در خشم رفت و مر او را به سیاهی بخشید که لب زبرینش از پرۀ بینی در گذشته بود و زیرینش به گریبان فرو هشته.

40. THEY having brought a Chinese girl to a certain king, whilst he was intoxicated, he wanted to have connection with her; but she refused compliance, at which he was so much enraged, that he gave her to one of his negro slaves... TALE XL. p. 166.

In the following stories, the reader will encounter the direct seen or visual evidentials signifying that the writer <u>has seen the theme of the story directly</u>. These stories are number

۵. سرهنگ زاده ای را بر در سرای اغلمش دیدم که عقل و کیاستی و فهم و فراستی زاید الوصف داشت هم از عهد خردی آثار بزرگی در ناصیه او پیدا.

5. I SAW at the gate of Ughulmish an officer's son, who was endowed with wisdom and sagacity beyond description: even his childhood was distinguished by proofs of superior abilities... TALE V. p. 121.

۱۰. بر بالین تربت یحیی پیغامبر علیه السلام معتکف بودم در جامع دمشق که یکی از ملوک عرب که به بی انصافی منسوب بود اتفاقاً به زیارت آمد و نماز و دعا کرد و حاجت خواست.

10. IN a certain year I was sitting retired in the great mosque at Damascus, at the head of the tomb of Yahiya the prophet (on whom be peace!)... TALE X. p. 127.

۱۴. یکی از پادشاهان پیشین در رعایت مملکت سستی کردی و لشکر به سختی داشتی لاجرم دشمنی صعب روی نهاد همه پشت بدادند.

14. ONE of the former kings was negligent in protecting his dominions, and having suffered his troops to be in distress, when a powerful

enemy appeared they forsook him. . . . I reproached him, saying "It is base, disreputable, mean, . . . TALE XIV. p. 132.

۱٦. کی از رفیقان شکایت روزگار نامساعد به نزد من آورد که کفاف اندک دارم و عیال بسیار و طاقت بار فاقه نمی‌آرم بارها در دلم آمد که به اقلیمی دیگر نقل کنم تا در هر آن صورت که زندگانی کرده شود کسی را بر نیک و بد من اطلاع نباشد.

16. ONE of my companions was complaining to me of the unfavorableness of the times, and said: "I have but small means with a large family, . . . TALE XVI. p. 134.

۱۷. تنی چند از روندگان در صحبت من بودند ظاهر ایشان به صلاح آراسته.

17. I WAS used to associate with a body of men, whose conduct had the appearance of correctness . . . TALE XVII. p. 140.

۳٥. با طایفه بزرگان به کشتی در نشسته بودم. زورقی در پی ما غرق شد. دو برادر به گردابی در افتادند.

35. I WAS sitting in a boat, in company with some persons of distinction, when a vessel near us sunk, and two brothers fell into a whirlpool . . . TALE XXXV. p. 162.

The **heard evidentials** (represented by the word "Shenidam": I heard, in the book) also will be found in the following stories:

۱. پادشاهی را شنیدم به کشتنِ اسیری اشارت کرد. بیچاره در آن حالت نومیدی ملک را دشنام دادن گرفت و سقط گفتن، که گفته‌اند هر که دست از جان بشوید، هر چه در دل دارد بگوید.

1. I HAVE heard, that a certain monarch having commanded a captive to be put to death, the poor wretch, in a fit of despair, . . . TALE I. p. 111

۳. ملک‌زاده ای را شنیدم که کوتاه بود و حقیر و دیگر برادران بلند و خوبروی، باری پدر به کراهت و استحقار در او نظر می‌کرد، پسر به فراست و استبصار به جای آورد . . .

3. I HEARD of a king's son, who was low in stature and ill-favored, whilst all his brothers were tall and handsome... TALE III. p. 114

٦. یکی را از ملوک عجم حکایت کنند که دست تطاول به مال رعیت دراز کرده بود و جور و اذیت آغاز کرده.

6. THEY tell a story of one of the kings of Persia, that he had stretched out the hand of oppression on the property of his subjects, and exercised tyranny and violence. TALE VI. P. 122

١٣. یکی از ملوک را شنیدم که شبی در عشرت روز کرده بود و در پایان مستی همی‌گفت...

13. I HEARD of a king, who had spent the night in jollity, and when he was completely intoxicated, he said, "I have never in my life .... TALE XIII. p. 130.

١٩. آورده‌اند که انوشیروان عادل را در شکارگاهی صید کباب کردند و نمک نبود غلامی به روستا رفت تا نمک آرد

19. THEY have related that Nowshirvan, being at a hunting seat, was about to have some game dressed, and as there was not any salt, a servant was sent to fetch some from a village... TALE XIX. p. 143.

٢٠. غافلی را شنیدم که خانه رعیت خراب کردی تا خزانه سلطان آباد کند بی خبر از قول حکیمان که گفته‌اند هر که خدای را عزّ و جلّ بیازارد تا دل خلقی به دست آرد خداوند تعالی همان خلق را بر او گمارد تا دمار از روزگارش بر آرد.

20. I HEARD of a collector of the revenues, who desolated the houses of the subjects, in order to fill the king's coffers; regardless of the maxim of the sages, which says, "Whosoever offendeth the Most High to gain the heart of a fellow-creature, God will make that very creature the instrument of his destruction."... TALE XX. p. 144.

٢١. مردم‌آزاری را حکایت کنند که سنگی بر سر صالحی زد. درویش را مجال انتقام نبود. سنگ را نگاه همی‌داشت تا زمانی که ملک را بر آن لشکری خشم آمد و در چاه کرد.

Evidentiality in Sa'dī's masterpieces 91

21. THEY tell a story of an oppressor, who flung a stone at the head of a pious man ... TALE XXI. p. 145.

۲٦. ظالمی را حکایت کنند که هیزم درویشان خریدی به حیف و توانگران را دادی به طرح، صاحبدلی بر او گذر کرد ...

26. THEY tell a story of an oppressor who purchased firewood from the poor by force, and gave it gratuitously to the rich ... TALE XXVI. p. 152.

۳۳. یکی از وزرا به زیردستان رحم کردی و صلاح ایشان را به خیر توسط نمودی.

33. THEY have related that a certain vizier had shown clemency towards those of an inferior decree, and had sought to accommodate every one ... TALE XXXIII. p. 160.

Quoted evidentials will be seen in the following tales:

۸. هرمز را گفتند وزیران پدر را چه خطا دیدی که بند فرمودی؟ گفت خطایی معلوم نکردم

8. THEY asked King Hormuz, "What crime have you found in your father's ministers, that you ordered them to be imprisoned?" TALE VIII. p. 125

۱۲. یکی از ملوک بی انصاف پارسایی را پرسید از عبادت‌ها کدام فاضل تر است؟ گفت تو را خواب نیم روز تا در آن یک نفس خلق را نیازاری.

12. A CERTAIN tyrannical king asked a religious man, "What kind of devotion will be most meritorious for me to perform ? ... TALE XII. p. 129.

۲۹. یکی از وزرا پیش ذوالنون مصری رفت و همت خواست که روز و شب به خدمت سلطان مشغولم و به خیرش امیدوار و از عقوبتش ترسان

29. A VIZIER went to Zool-noon of Egypt, and, asking his blessing, said, "I am day and night employed in the service of the king, hoping for

۳۹. هارون الرشید را چون ملک دیار مصر مسلم شد گفت: به خلاف آن طاغی که به غرور ملک مصر دعوی خدایی کرد نبخشم این مملکت را مگر به خسیس‌ترین بندگان.

39. HAROONur Rusheed, when he had completed the conquest of Egypt, said, "As a contrast to that rebel, who, through the pride of his possessing the kingdom of Egypt, boasted that he was God, I will bestow this kingdom on the meanest of my slaves." ... TALE XXXIX. p. 165.

٤١. اسکندر رومی را پرسیدند: دیار مشرق و مغرب به چه گرفتی که ملوک پیشین را خزاین و عمر و ملک و لشکر بیش از این بوده است و ایشان را چنین فتحی میسر نشده.

41. THEY asked Alexander the Great, "By what means have you extended your conquests from east to west, since former monarchs, who exceeded you in wealth, in territory, in years, and in the number of troops, never gained such victories?" .... TALE XLI. p. 168.

Overall, in the first chapter, unknown evidentials, heard evidentials, and visual evidentials are used respectively in terms of frequency of occurrence.

CHAPTER 2 OF *GOLESTĀN*

The second chapter of *Golestān*, called "On the Morals of Durwaishes," contains 47 tales (see Table 3.14).

In some stories of this chapter you will see that there is **no known evidential**, meaning the reader won't know how Sa'dī exactly knows the story and what

Table 3.14 Frequency of evidentials in second chapter of *Golestān*

Chapter	Episodes without evidentials		Episodes with evidentials			
	Advice	Unknown source	Direct visual evidence	Heard	Quotation	Inferred/ assumed
2 Number of cases	–	21	15	1	10	–

his source of information is. These stories include the stories specified by the exact numbers of

٤. دزدی به خانهٔ پارسایی در آمد. چندان که جست چیزی نیافت. دلتنگ شد. پارسا خبر شد. گلیمی که بر آن خفته بود در راه دزد انداخت تا محروم نشود.

4. A THIEF got into the house of a religious man, but, after the most diligent search, had the mortification not to find anything ... TALE IV. p. 171.

٦. زاهدی مهمان پادشاهی بود. چون به طعام بنشستند کمتر از آن خورد که ارادت او بود و چون به نماز برخاستند بیش از آن کرد که عادت او، تا ظنّ صلاحیت در حق او زیادت کنند.

6. A ZAHID was invited to a feast by a king; when he sat down at the table, he ate more sparingly than he was accustomed to do; and when he stood up to prayers, he was longer than usual; ... TALE VI. p. 174.

٩. یکی از صلحای لبنان که مقامات او در دیار عرب مذکور بود و کرامات مشهور به جامع دمشق در آمد و بر کنار برکه کلاسه طهارت همی‌ساخت. پایش بلغزید و به حوض در افتاد و به مشقت از آن جایگه خلاص یافت.

9. ONE of the religious men of Mount Libanus, whose piety and miracles were famed throughout Arabia, entered the great mosque of Damascus, and was purifying himself on the edge of the cistern of the well, when, his feet slipping, he fell into the water, and with great difficulty got out of it ... TALE IX. p. 176.

١٤. درویشی را ضرورتی پیش آمد، گلیمی از خانه یاری بدزدید. حاکم فرمود که دستش بدر کنند. صاحب گلیم شفاعت کرد که: من او را بحل کردم.

14. A DURWAISH, having some pressing occasion, stole a blanket from the house of a friend. The judge ordered that they should cut off his hand. The owner of the blanket interceded, and said that he absolved him ... TALE XIV. p. 181.

١٥. یکی از جمله صالحان به خواب دید پادشاهی را در بهشت و پارسایی در دوزخ. پرسید که موجب درجات این چیست و سبب درکات آن که مردم به خلاف این معتقد بودند؟

15. A CERTAIN pious man saw in a dream a king in paradise, and a holy man in hell; he asked what could be the meaning of the exaltation of one, and the degradation of the other, as the contrary is generally considered to be the case ? TALE XVI. p. 183.

۱۷. زاهدی مهمان پادشاهی بود. چون به طعام بنشستند کمتر از آن خورد که ارادت او بود و چون به نماز برخاستند بیش از آن کرد که عادت او، تا ظنّ صلاحیت در حق او زیادت کنند.

17. A CERTAIN king sent an invitation to a religious man. He thought by taking medicine to make himself weak, in order that the king might entertain a high opinion of him ... TALE XVIII. p. 184.

۱۸. کاروانی در زمین یونان بزدند و نعمت بی قیاس ببردند. بازرگانان گریه و زاری کردند و خدا و پیمبر شفیع آوردند و فایده نبود

18. IN the land of Greece a caravan was attacked by robbers, and plundered of immense wealth. The merchants made grievous lamentations, and besought them by God and his Prophet, but without effect ... TALE XIX. p. 183.

۲۲. بخشایش الهی گم شده‌ای را در مناهی چراغ توفیق فرا راه داشت تا به حلقه اهل تحقیق در آمد. به یمن قدم درویشان و صدق نفس ایشان ذمائم اخلاقش به حمائد مبدل گشت دست از هوا و هوس کوتاه کرده و زبان طاعنان در حق او همچنان دراز که بر قاعده اوّل است و زهد و طاعتش نامعوّل.

22. TO one who through wickedness had forfeited the divine favor, the lamp of grace shone on his path, whereby he entered into the circle of the religious; and, by the blessing of their society and righteousness, his depravities were exchanged for virtuous deeds, and he ceased to entertain any sensual inclinations: nevertheless, the tongue of calumny was still exercised on his character; his former manners being remembered, and no credit given to his piety and virtues. TALE XXIII. p. 190.

۲۷. یکی را از ملوک مدّت عمر سپری شد. قائم مقامی نداشت. وصیت کرد که بامدادان نخستین کسی که از در شهر اندر آید تاج شاهی بر سر وی نهند و تفویض مملکت بدو کنند.

27. A CERTAIN king, when arrived at the end of his days, having no heir, directed in his will, that in the morning after his death, the first person who entered the gate of the city, they should place on his head the crown of royalty, and commit to his charge the government of the kingdom... TALE XXVIII. p. 195.

۲۸. یکی را دوستی بود که عمل دیوان کردی. مدتی اتفاق دیدن نیفتاد. کسی گفت: فلانرا دیر شد که ندیدی. گفت: من او را نخواهم که ببینم. قضا را یکی از کسان او حاضر بود.

28. A CERTAIN person had a friend employed in the office of Dewan, with whom he had not chanced to meet for some time. Somebody said to him, "It is a long time since you saw such a one." He answered, "Neither do I wish to see him." It happened that one of the Dewan's people was present, who asked what fault his friend had been guilty of, that he was not inclined to see him... TALE XXIX. p. 197.

۲۹. یکی را از بزرگان بادی مخالف در شکم پیچیدن گرفت و طاقت ضبط آن نداشت و بی اختیار از او صادر شد. گفت ای دوستان مرا در آنچه کردم اختیاری نبود و بزهی بر من ننوشتند و راحتی به وجود من رسید. شما هم به کرم معذور دارید.

29. One of the greatest man was experiencing cramp and he could not tolerate it... TALE XXX. p. 197.

۳۱. یکی از پادشاهان عابدی را پرسید -که عیالان داشت-: اوقات عزیز چگونه می‌گذرد؟ گفت: همه شب در مناجات و سحر در دعای حاجات و همه روز در بند اخراجات.

31. A CERTAIN king asked a religious man how he passed his valuable time; he replied, "All night I pray, in the morning I offer up my vows and petitions, and the whole day is spent in regulating my expenses." ... TALE XXXII. p. 200.

۳۲. یکی از متعبّدان در بیشه زندگانی کردی و برگ درختان خوردی. پادشاهی به حکم زیارت به نزدیک وی رفت و گفت: اگر مصلحت بینی به شهر اندر برای تو مقامی بسازم که فراغ عبادت از این به دست دهد و دیگران هم به برکت انفاس شما مستفید گردند و به صلاح اعمال شما اقتدا کنند.

32. ONE of the hermits of Damascus had passed many years in the desert, in devotion, feeding on the leaves of trees. The king of that country, having gone to visit him, said, "It seems advisable to me that I should prepare a place for you in the city, where you may perform your devotions more conveniently, and others be benefited by the blessing of your company, and take example from your goodworks." The hermit would not consent to this proposal... TALE XXXIII. p. 200.

۳۳. مطابق این سخن پادشاهی را مهمی پیش آمد. گفت اگر این حالت به مراد من بر آید چندین درم دهم زاهدان را. چون حاجتش بر آمد و تشویش خاطرش برفت وفای نذرش به وجود شرط لازم آمد. یکی را از بندگان خاص کیسه درم داد تا صرف کند بر زاهدان.

33. THE following story will exemplify what has been said above. A king, having some weighty affairs in agitation, made a vow that, in case of success, he would distribute a certain sum of money amongst men dedicated to religion... TALE XXXIV. p. 204.

۳۵. درویشی به مقامی در آمد که صاحب آن بقعه کریم النفس بود. طایفه اهل فضل و بلاغت در صحبت او هر یکی بذله و لطیفه همی‌گفتند. درویش راه بیابان کرده بود و مانده و چیزی نخورده.

35. A DURWAISH came to a place where the master of the house was of a hospitable disposition. The company consisted of persons of understanding and eloquence, who separately delivered a joke or pleasantry in a manner becoming men of wit... TALE XXXVI. p. 205.

۳۸. یکی بر سر راهی مست خفته بود و زمام اختیار از دست رفته. عابدی بر وی گذر کرد و در آن حالت مستقبح او نظر کرد.

38. A DRUNKEN man was sleeping on the highway, overcome by the power of intoxication a devotee passed by, and beheld his condition with detestation. The young man lifted up his head and said:
 "When you meet an inconsiderate person, pass him with kindness; and when you see a sinner, conceal his crime, and be compassionate."... TALE XL. p. 208.

٤٠. این حکایت شنو که در بغداد/ رایت و پرده را خلاف افتاد
رایت از گرد راه و رنج رکاب/ گفت با پرده از طریق عتاب:
من و تو هر دو خواجه‌تاشانیم/ بندهٔ بارگاه سلطانیم

40. ATTEND to the following story. In the city of Baghdad there happened a contention between the flag and the curtain ... TALE XLII. p. 210.

۴۱. یکی از صاحبدلان زورآزمایی را دید به هم برآمده و کف بر دماغ انداخته.
گفت: این را چه حالت است؟
گفتند: فلان دشنامم دادش.

41. HOLY man saw a wrestler distracted and foaming at the mouth with rage: he inquired the cause, and was told some one had given him abuse ... TALE XLIII. p. 211.

۴۳. پیرمردی لطیف در بغداد/ دخترک را به کفشدوزی داد
مردک سنگدل چنان بگزید/ لب دختر که خون از او بچکید
بامدادان پدر چنان دیدش/ پیش داماد رفت و پرسیدش

43. A MERRY fellow of Baghdad married his daughter to a shoemaker. The little man, having a flinty heart, bit the girl's lips in such a manner, that they trickled with blood ... TALE XLV. p. 213.

۴۴. آورده‌اند که فقیهی دختری داشت به غایت زشت به جای زنان رسیده و با وجود جهاز و نعمت کسی در مناکحت او رغبت نمی‌نمود.

44. A CERTAIN lawyer had a very ugly daughter, who was marriageable; but although he offered a considerable dower, and other valuables, no one was inclined to wed her ... TALE XLVI. p. 213.

۴۵. ادشاهی به دیده استحقار در طایفه درویشان نظر کرد. یکی ز آن میان به فراست به جای آورد و گفت: ای ملک! ما در این دنیا به جیش از تو کمتریم و به عیش خوشتر و به مرگ برابر و به قیامت بهتر.

45. A CERTAIN king regarded with contempt the society of Durwaishes, which one of them having the penetration to discover, said, "O king! In this world you have the advantage of us in external grandeur, but with regard to the comforts of life we are your superiors; at the time of death we shall be your equals; and at the resurrection our state will be preferable to yours." ... TALE XLVII. p. 214.

In some stories, the reader will encounter the **seen visual evidentials** signifying that the writer has seen the theme of the story directly. These stories are number

۲. درویشی را دیدم سر بر آستان کعبه همی‌مالید و می‌گفت: یا غفور یا رحیم
تو دانی که از ظلوم و جهول چه آید.

2. I SAW a Durwaish, who, having placed his forehead on the threshold of the temple of Mecca, was lamenting and saying: "O gracious and most merciful God, thou knowest what can ... TALE II. p. 169.

۵. تنی چند از روندگان متفق سیاحت بودند و شریک رنج و راحت. خواستم تا مرافقت کنم موافقت نکردند. گفتم: این از کرم اخلاق بزرگان بدیع است روی از مصاحبت مسکینان تافتن و فایده و برکت دریغ داشتن، که من در نفس خویش این قدرت و سرعت می‌شناسم که در خدمت مردان یار شاطر باشم نه بار خاطر.

5. SOME travelers were journeying together, partakers of each other's cares and comforts; I wanted to associate myself with them, to which they would not consent. I remarked that it was inconsistent with the benevolent manners of religious men, to turn away their faces from the poor, and to deny them the advantage of such company ... TALE V. p. 172.

۷. یاد دارم که در ایام طفولیت متعبد بودمی و شب خیز و مولع زهد و پرهیز. شبی در خدمت پدر رحمة الله علیه نشسته بودم و همه شب دیده بر هم نبسته و مصحف عزیز بر کنار گرفته و طایفه‌ای گرد ما خفته.

7. I REMEMBER that in the time of childhood I was very religious: I rose in the night, was punctual in the performance of my devotions, and abstinent ... TALE VII. p. 175.

۱۰. در جامع بعلبک وقتی کلمه‌ای همی‌گفتم به طریق وعظ با جماعتی افسرده دل مرده ره از عالم صورت به عالم معنی نبرده. دیدم که نفسم در نمی‌گیرد و آتشم در هیزم تر اثر نمی‌کند.

10. IN the great mosque at Balbuk I was reciting some words by way of admonition to a company whose hearts were withered and dead, inca-

pable of applying the ways of the visible to the purposes of the invisible world... TALE XI. p. 179.

۱۱. شبی در بیابان مکه از بی‌خوابی پای رفتنم نماند. سر بنهادم و شتربان را گفتم دست از من بدار.

11. ONE night, in the desert of Mecca, from the great want of sleep, I was deprived of all power to stir; I reclined my head on the earth, and desired the camel-driver not to disturb me... TALE XII. p. 180.

۱۲. پارسایی را دیدم بر کنار دریا که زخم پلنگ داشت و به هیچ دارو به نمی‌شد. مدتها در آن رنجور بود و شکر خدای عزّوجل علی الدوام گفتی. پرسیدندش که شکر چه می‌گویی؟ گفت: شکر آن که به مصیبتی گرفتارم نه به معصیتی.

12. I SAW on the sea-shore a religious man, who had a wound from a tiger, which could not be cured by any medicine... TALE XIII. p. 181.

۱٦. پیاده‌ای سر و پا برهنه با کاروان حجاز از کوفه به در آمد و همراه ما شد و معلوم می نداشت.
خرامان همی‌رفت و می‌گفت: نه به استر بر سوارم نه چو اشتر زیر بارم/ نه خداوند رعیت نه غلام شهریارم

16. A FOOT traveler, bareheaded, and without shoes, came from Cufeh, and accompanied [us] the caravan to Mecca... TALE XVII. p. 183.

۲۰. چندان که مرا شیخ اجلّ ابوالفرج بن جوزی رحمة الله علیه ترک سماع فرمودی و به خلوت و عزلت اشارت کردی عنفوان شبابم غالب آمدی و هوا و هوس طالب. ناچار به خلاف رای مربّی قدمی برفتمی و از سماع و مجالست حظی برگرفتمی و چون نصیحت شیخم یاد آمدی گفتمی:
قاضی ار با ما نشیند برفشاند دست را/ محتسب گر می خورد معذور دارد مست را

19. NOT WITHSTANDING all that was said to me by Sheik Shumsuddeen Abulfureh Ben Jowzee, who ordered me to forsake music meetings, and to lead a life of retirement, the spring-tide of youth prevailed, the desire of sensual gratification not admitting of restraint; and, in contradiction

to the advice of my patron, I abandoned myself to the enjoyments of singing and of convivial society . . . TALE XX. p. 186.

٢٣. پیش یکی از مشایخ گله کردم که: فلان به فساد من گواهی داده است. گفتا: به صلاحش خجل کن!

23. LAMENTED to a venerable Sheik, that someone had accused me falsely of lasciviousness. He replied, "Put him to shame by your virtue . . . TALE XXIV. p. 191.

٢٥. یاد دارم که شبی در کاروانی همه شب رفته بودم و سحر در کنار بیشه‌ای خفته. شوریده‌ای که در آن سفر همراه ما بود نعره‌ای برآورد و راه بیابان گرفت و یک نفس آرام نیافت. چون روز شد گفتمش: آن چه حالت بود؟

25. I RECOLLECT that once I had travelled the whole night with the caravan, and in the morning had gone to sleep by the side of a desert . . . TALE XXVI. p. 192.

٢٦. وقتی در سفر حجاز طایفه‌ای جوانان صاحبدل همدم من بودند و هم قدم. وقت‌ها زمزمه‌ای بکردندی و بیتی محققانه بگفتندی، و عابدی در سبیل منکر حال درویشان بود و بی‌خبر از درد ایشان.

26. ONCE I travelled to Hejaz along with some young men of virtuous disposition, who had been my intimate friends and constant companions . . . TALE XXVII. p. 193.

٣٠. از صحبت یاران دمشقم ملالتی پدید آمده بود. سر در بیابان قدس نهادم و با حیوانات انس گرفتم.
تا وقتی که اسیر فرنگ شدم و در خندق طرابلس با جهودانم به کار گل بداشتند.

30. HAVING become weary of the company of my friends at Damascus, I retired into the desert of Jerusalem, and associated with the brutes, till I was taken prisoner by the Franks, and consigned to a pit in Tripoli, to dig clay, along with some Jews . . . TALE XXXI. p. 198.

٣٦. مریدی گفت پیر را: چه کنم کز خلایق به رنج اندرم از بس که به زیارت من همی‌آیند و اوقات مرا از تردّد ایشان تشویش می‌باشد؟ گفت: هر چه

درویشانند مر ایشان را وامی بده و آنچه توانگرانند از ایشان چیزی بخواه که دیگر یکی گرد تو نگردند !
گر گدا پیشرو لشکر اسلام بود / کافر از بیم توقع برود تا در چین

36. A PUPIL complained to his spiritual guide of being much disturbed by impertinent visitors, who broke in upon his valuable time, and he asked how he could get rid of them.The superior replied: "To such of them as are poor, lend money, and from those that are rich ask something, when you may depend upon not seeing one of them again. If a beggar was the leader of the army of Islamism, the infidels would flee to China through fear of his importunity."... TALE XXXVII. p. 206.

۳۹. طایفه رندان به خلاف درویشی به در آمدند و سخنان ناسزا گفتند و بزدند و برنجانیدند. شکایت از بی‌طاقتی پیش پیر طریقت برد که چنین حالی رفت.

39. A COMPANY of dissolute men came to dispute with a Durwaish, and made use of improper expressions; at which being offended, he went to his spiritual guide, and complained of what had happened ... TALE XLI. p. 209.

٤٦. دیدم گل تازه چند دسته /بر گنبدی از گیاه رسته

46. I SAW some nosegays of fresh roses tied to a dome with some grass. I said, "What is this worthless grass, that it should thus be in the company of roses?"... TALE XLVIII. p. 216.

The heard evidentials also will be found in stories number

۲۱. عابدی را حکایت کنند که شبی ده من طعام بخوردی و تا سحر ختمی در نماز بکردی. صاحبدلی شنید و گفت: اگر نیم نانی بخوردی و بخفتی بسیار از این فاضل‌تر بودی.

21. THEY tell a story of a certain religious man, who in one night would eat ten pounds of food, and who before the morning would have completely finished the Koran in his devotions. A holy man hearing this, said, "If he had eaten half a loaf, and slept, it would have been much more meritorious."... TALE XXII. p. 189.

Quoted evidentials will be seen in the following tales

١. یکی از بزرگان گفت پارسایی را: چه گویی در حق فلان عابد که دیگران در حق وی به طعنه سخن‌ها گفته‌اند؟ گفت: بر ظاهرش عیب نمی‌بینم و در باطنش غیب نمی‌دانم.

1. A CERTAIN personage asked a devout man what he said of a particular Abid, of whose character others had spoken disrespectfully . . . TALE I. p. 169.

٣. عبدالقادر گیلانی را رحمة الله علیه دیدند در حرم کعبه روی بر حصبا نهاده همی‌گفت: ای خداوند ببخشای! وگر هر آینه مستوجب عقوبتم در روز قیامتم نابینا برانگیز تا در روی نیکان شرمسار نشوم.

3. UBDULKADUR Gilanee, [was seen] having placed his forehead on the pebbles before the gate of the temple of Mecca, was saying, "O God, pardon my sins; . . . TALE III. p. 170.

٨. یکی را از بزرگان به محفلی اندر همی‌ستودند و در اوصاف جمیلش مبالغه می‌کردند.
سر بر آورد و گفت: من آنم که من دانم.

8. IN a company where every one was praising a religious man, and extolling his virtues, he raised up his head, and said: "I am such as I know myself to be, whilst thou who reckonest up my good works judgest from the external, but art ignorant of the interior . . . TALE VIII. p. 176.

١٤. پادشاهی پارسایی را دید.
گفت: هیچت از ما یاد آید؟
گفت: بلی! وقتی که خدا را فراموش می‌کنم.

14. CERTAIN king said to a religious man, "Do you ever think of me?" He answered, "Yes, whenever I forget God." He fleeth everywhere whom God driveth from his gate; but whomsoever God inviteth, he will not suffer to run to the door of any one . . . TALE XV. p. 182.

٢١. لقمان را گفتند: ادب از که آموختی؟
گفت: از بی ادبان! هر چه از ایشان در نظرم ناپسند آمد از فعل آن پرهیز کردم.

20. THEY asked Lokman from whom he had learnt urbanity; he replied, "From those of rude manners; for whatsoever I saw in them that was disagreeable, I avoided doing the same . . . TALE XXI. p. 189.

۲٤. یکی را از مشایخ شام پرسیدند از حقیقت تصوف. گفت: پیش از این طایفه‌ای در جهان بودند به صورت پریشان و به معنی جمع، اکنون جماعتی هستند به صورت جمع و به معنی پریشان.

24. THEY asked one of the Sheiks of Damascus what was the condition of the sect of Soofies? He replied: "They formerly were, in the world, a society of men apparently in distress, but in reality contented; but now they are a tribe in appearance satisfied, but inwardly discontented." . . . TALE XXV. p. 192.

۳٤. یکی را از علمای راسخ پرسیدند: چه گویی در نان وقف؟ گفت: اگر نان از بهر جمعیت خاطر می‌ستاند حلال است و اگر جمع از بهر نان می‌نشیند حرام.

34. THEY asked a certain wise man, what was his opinion of consecrated bread? He replied: "If they receive it in order to compose their minds, and to promote their devotions, it is awful; but if they want nothing but bread, it is illegal. Men of piety receive bread to enjoy religious retirement, but enter not into the cell of devotion for the sake of obtaining bread." . . . TALE XXXV. p. 205.

۳۷. فقیهی پدر را گفت: هیچ از این سخنان رنگین دلاویز متکلمان در من اثر نمی‌کند به حکم آن که نمی‌بینم مر ایشان را فعلی موافق گفتار: ترک دنیا به مردم آموزند / خویشتن سیم و غلّه اندوزند

37. A LAWYER said to his father: "Those fine speeches of the declaimers make no impression on me, because I do not see that their actions correspond with their precepts. They teach people to forsake the world, whilst themselves accumulate property . . . TALE XXXVIII. p. 207.

٤۲. بزرگی را پرسیدم از سیرت اخوان صفا. گفت: کمینه آن که مراد خاطر یاران بر مصالح خویش مقدّم دارد و حکما گفته‌اند: برادر که در بند خویش است نه برادر و نه خویش است.

42. THEY interrogated a learned man concerning; the character of his brethren, the Sufis. He answered:

"The meanest of their excellences is, that they prefer gratifying the desire of their friends to attending to their own... TALE XL IV. p. 211.

٤٧. حکیمی را پرسیدند: از سخاوت و شجاعت کدام بهتر است؟
گفت: آن که را سخاوت است به شجاعت حاجت نیست.

47. THEY asked a wise man which was preferable, fortitude or liberality? He replied: "He who possesseth liberality hath no need of fortitude. It is inscribed on the tomb of Bahram Goar, that a liberal and is preferable to a strong arm." Hatim Tai no longer exists; but his exalted name will remain famous for virtue to eternity. Distribute the tithes of your wealth in alms, for when the husband man lops off the exuberant branches from the vine, it produces an increase of grapes... TALE XLIX. p. 217.

In this chapter there won't be found any story that is the direct or indirect quotation of a specific person or source of knowledge. Overall, one can say that in this chapter unknown evidentials, visual, evidentials, and heard evidentials are used respectively in terms of frequency of occurrence.

CHAPTER 3 OF *GOLESTĀN*

The third chapter of *Golestān*, called "Of the Excellency of Contentment," contains 29 stories (see Table 3.15).

In 18 stories of this chapter you will see that there is **no known evidential**. These stories include the stories specified by the exact number of

۲. و امیرزاده در مصر بودند. یکی علم آموخت و دیگر مال اندوخت. عاقبة الأمر آن یکی علّامه عصر گشت و این یکی عزیز مصر شد.

Table 3.15 Frequency of evidentials in third chapter of *Golestān*

Chapter	Episodes without evidentials		Episodes with evidentials			
	Advice	Unknown source	Direct visual evidence	Heard	Quotation	Inferred/ assumed
3 Number of cases	–	12	5	6	6	–

2. IN Egypt dwelt two sons of a nobleman, one of whom acquired learning, and the other gained wealth; the former became the most learned man of his time, and the other prince of Egypt... TALE II. p. 218.

٤. یکی از ملوک عجم طبیبی حاذق به خدمت مصطفی صلی الله علیه و سلم فرستاد. سالی در دیار عرب بود و کسی تجربه پیش او نیاورد و معالجه از وی در نخواست.

4. ONE of the kings of Persia sent a skillful physician to Mustufa, upon whom be peace! He had been some years in Arabia without anyone having come to make trial of his skill, neither had they applied to him for any medicine... TALE IV. p. 220.

٦. دو درویش خراسانی ملازم صحبت یکدیگر سفر کردندی. یکی ضعیف بود که هر بدو شب افطار کردی و دیگر قوی که روزی سه بار خوردی.

6. TWO Durwaishes of Khorasan, who had entered into strict intimacy, travelled together; one, who was infirm, would fast for two days, and the other, who was robust, used to eat three times a day... TALE VII. p. 222.

٩. بقالی را درمی چند بر صوفیان گرد آمده بود در واسط. هر روز مطالبت کردی و سخنان با خشونت گفتی.

9. A BUTCHER in the city of Wasit, to whom the Sufis had contracted some debts, was every day importuning them for payment, and made use of very harsh language... TALE X. p. 224.

١٠. جوانمردی را در جنگ تاتار جراحتی هول رسید. کسی گفت: فلان بازرگان نوشدارو دارد. اگر بخواهی باشد که دریغ ندارد. گویند آن بازرگان به بخل معروف بود.

10. A CERTAIN gallant man was grievously wounded in an expedition against the Tartars; somebody said, Such a merchant has an unguent, of which perhaps he might give you a little were you to ask it... TALE XI. p. 225.

١١. یکی از علما خورندهٔ بسیار داشت و کفاف اندک. یکی را از بزرگان که در او معتقد بود بگفت. روی از توقع او در هم کشید و تعرّض سؤال از اهل ادب در نظرش قبیح آمد.

11. A CERTAIN learned man who had a large family to support, with very scanty means, represented his case to a great man who entertained a favorable opinion of him.... TALE XII. p. 226.

۱۳. خشکسالی در اسکندریه عنان طاقت درویش از دست رفته بود، درهای آسمان بر زمین بسته و فریاد اهل زمین به آسمان پیوسته.

13. THERE happened one year such a drought at Alexandria, that men could not support it with patience; the doors of heaven were shut against the earth, and the lamentations of all creatures reached the sky... TALE XIV. p. 228.

۱۵. موسی علیه السلام درویشی را دید از برهنگی به ریگ اندر شده. گفت: ای موسی! دعا کن تا خدا عزّوجلّ مرا کفافی دهد که از بی طاقتی به جان آمدم. موسی دعا کرد و برفت.

15. MOSES the prophet, upon whom be peace! saw a Durwaish, who, for want of clothes, had hidden himself in the sand; he said, "O Moses, implore God to bestow on me a subsistence, for I am perishing in distress." Moses prayed, and God granted him assistance... TALE XVI. p. 230.

۱۸. همچنین در قاع بسیط مسافری گم شده بود و قوت و قوّتش به آخر آمده و درمی چند بر میان داشت. بسیاری بگردید و ره به جایی نبرد.

18. A darvish was lost in Gha'e Basit and he was run out of food and there remained some Dinars for him...... TALE XVII. p. 231.

۲۰. یکی از ملوک با تنی چند خاصان در شکارگاهی به زمستان از عمارت دور افتادند، تا شب در آمد خانهٔ دهقانی دیدند.

20. A CERTAIN king, attended by some of his principal nobility, on a hunting party, in the winter, was benighted at a long distance from any town. Having discovered the cottage of a peasant, the king said, "Let us go there for the night, that we may not suffer inconvenience from the cold."... TALE XX. p. 233.

۲۵. دست و پا بریده‌ای هزارپایی بکشت. صاحبدلی بر او گذر کرد و گفت: سبحان الله! با هزار پای که داشت چون اجلش فرا رسید از بی دست و پایی گریختن نتوانست.

Evidentiality in Sa'dī's masterpieces 107

25. ONE who had neither hands nor feet having killed a milleped, a pious man passing by said, "Holy God, although this had a thousand feet, yet when fate overtook him he could not escape from one destitute of hands and feet." ... TALE XXV. p. 240.

۲۷. دزدی گدایی را گفت: شرم نداری که دست از برای جوی سیم پیش هر لئیم دراز میکنی؟ گفت : دست دراز از پی یک حبه سیم /به که ببرند به دانگی و نیم

27. A THIEF said to a mendicant, "Are you not ashamed to hold out your hand to every sordid wretch to obtain a grain of silver?" He replied, "It is better to stretch out the hand for a grain of silver, than to have it cut off for having stolen a dang and a half." ... TALE XXVII. p. 241.

In some stories the reader will encounter the **visual/seen evidentials** signifying that the writer has seen the theme of the story directly. These stories are number

۱۶. اعرابیی را دیدم در حلقهٔ جوهریان بصره که حکایت همی‌کرد که: وقتی در بیابانی راه گم کرده بودم و از زاد معنی چیزی با من نمانده بود و دل بر هلاک نهاده، که همی ناگاه کیسه‌ای یافتم پر مروارید. هرگز آن ذوق و شادی فراموش نکنم که پنداشتم گندم بریان است، باز آن تلخی و نومیدی که معلوم کردم که مروارید است!

16. I SAW an Arab sitting in a circle of jewelers of Basrah, and relating as follows: "Once on a time, having missed my way in the desert, and having no provisions left, I gave myself up for lost: when I happened to find a bag full of pearls, I shall never forget the relish and delight that I felt on supposing it to be fried wheat; nor the bitterness and despair which I suffered, on discovering that the bag contained pearls ... TALE XVII. p. 231.

۱۹. هرگز از دور زمان ننالیده بودم و روی از گردش آسمان در هم نکشیده، مگر وقتی که پایم برهنه مانده بود و استطاعت پای پوشی نداشتم. به جامع کوفه در آمدم دلتنگ، یکی را دیدم که پای نداشت. سپاس نعمت حق به جای آوردم و بر بی کفشی صبر کردم.

19. I NEVER complained of the vicissitudes of fortune, nor murmured at the ordinances of Heaven, excepting once, when my feet were,

and I had not the means of procuring myself shoes . . . TALE XIX. p. 233.

۲۲. بازرگانی را شنیدم که صد و پنجاه شتر بار داشت و چهل بنده خدمتکار. شبی در جزیره کیش مرا به حجره خویش در آورد.

22. I SAW a merchant who possessed one hundred and fifty camels laden with merchandise, and fifty slaves and servants . . . TALE XXII. p. 236.

۲۶. ابلهی را دیدم سمین، خلعتی ثمین در بر و مرکبی تازی در زیر و قصبی مصری بر سر.
کسی گفت: سعدی! چگونه می‌بینی این دیبای مُعلَّم بر این حیوان لا یعلَمْ؟

26. I SAW a fat blockhead clad in a rich dress and mounted on an Arab horse, with fine Egyptian linen round his head. Someone said, "O Sādi, what is your opinion of this notable dress on this ignorant brute?" . . . TALE XXVI. p. 240.

۲۷. درویشی را دیدم که به غاری در نشسته بود و در به روی از جهانیان بسته و ملوک و اغنیا را در چشم همت او شوکت و هیبت نمانده.

29. I SAW a Durwaish, who, having seated himself in a cave, had given up worldly society, regarding neither kings nor princes . . . TALE XXIX. p. 254.

The **heard evidentials** also will be found in stories number

۳. درویشی را شنیدم که در آتش فاقه می‌سوخت و رقعه بر خرقه می‌دوخت و تسکین خاطر مسکین را همی‌گفت:
به نان خشک قناعت کنیم و جامه دلق/ که بار محنت خود به که بار منت خلق

3. I HEARD of a Durwaish who was suffering great distress from poverty, and sewing patch upon patch, but who comforted himself with the following verse: "I am contented with stale bread, and a coarse woollen frock, since it is better to bear the weight of one's own necessities than to suffer the load of obligation from mankind." . . . TALE III. p. 219.

۵. در سیرت اردشیر بابکان آمده است که حکیم عرب را پرسید که: روزی چه مایه طعام باید خوردن؟
گفت: صد درم سنگ کفایت است.

5. IN the annals of Ardsheer Babukan, it is recorded, that he asked an Arabian physician, what quantity of food ought to be eaten in the course of a day. He answered, that the weight of one hundred direms was sufficient... TALE VI. p. 222.

۲۱. گدایی هول را حکایت کنند که نعمتی وافر اندوخته بود. یکی از پادشاهان گفتش: همی‌نمایند که مال بی کران داری و ما را مهمی هست، اگر به برخی از آن دستگیری کنی چون ارتفاع رسد وفا کرده شود و شکر گفته.

21. THEY tell a story of a horrible mendicant, who was possessed of considerable wealth. A certain king said to him, "It appears that you are exceedingly rich, and as I have a pressing demand, if you will assist me with a small... TALE XXI. p. 234.

۲۳. مالداری را شنیدم که به بخل چنان معروف بود که حاتم طایی در کرم. ظاهر حالش به نعمت دنیا آراسته و خست نفس جبلی در وی همچنان متمکن، تا به جایی که نانی به جانی از دست ندادی و گربهٔ بوهریره را به لقمه‌ای ننواختی و سگ اصحاب الکهف را استخوانی نینداختی.

23. I HEARD of a certain rich man, who was as notorious for parsimony as Hatim Tai for liberality... TALE XXIII. p. 237.

۲٤. صیادی ضعیف را ماهی قوی به دام اندر افتاد. طاقت حفظ آن نداشت، ماهی بر او غالب آمد و دام از دستش در ربود و برفت.

24. *[I HEARD]* A POWERFUL fish fell into the net of a debilitated fisherman, who not being able to hold it, the fish got the better of him, snatched the net out of his hand, and escaped... TALE XXIV. p. 239.

۲۸. مشت‌زنی را حکایت کنند که از دهر مخالف به فغان آمده و حلق فراخ از دست تنگ به جان رسیده شکایت پیش پدر برد و اجازت خواست که: عزم سفر دارم، مگر به قوت بازو دامن کامی فرا چنگ آرم.

28. THEY tell a story of a wrestler, who from adverse fortune was reduced to the extremity of misery... TALE XXVIII. p. 241.

Quoted evidentials

۱. خواهنده مغربی در صفِّ بزّازان حلب می‌گفت: ای خداوندان نعمت، اگر شما را انصاف بودی و ما را قناعت، رسم سؤال از جهان برخاستی.
ای قناعت! توانگرم گردان/ که ورای تو هیچ نعمت نیست
کنج صبر اختیار لقمان است/ هر که را صبر نیست حکمت نیست

1. AN African mendicant at Aleppo, in the quarter occupied by the dealers in linen cloths, was saying, "O wealthy Sirs, if there had been justice amongst you, and we had possessed contentment, there would have been an end of beggary in this world." O contentment, make me rich! For without thee there is no wealth. Lokman made choice of patience in retirement. Whosoever hath not patience, neither doth he possess philosophy... TALE I. p. 218.

۷. یکی از حکما پسر را نهی می‌کرد از بسیار خوردن که سیری مردم را رنجور کند.
گفت: ای پدر! گرسنگی خلق را بکشد، نشنیده‌ای که ظریفان گفته‌اند به سیری مردن به که گرسنگی بردن.

7. A CERTAIN wise man admonished his son against eating to excess, because repletion occasions sickness. The son answered, "O father! hunger killeth; and have you not heard the saying of the sages, that it is better to die of excess, than to suffer the pangs of hunger? The father replied, "Be moderate, for God hath said, Eat ye and drink, but not to excess... TALE VIII. p. 223.

۸. رنجوری را گفتند: دلت چه می‌خواهد؟ گفت: آن که دلم چیزی نخواهد.
معده چو کج گشت و شکم درد خاست / سود ندارد همه اسباب راست

8. THEY asked a sick man, what his heart desired? He replied, "Only this, that it may not desire anything." When the stomach is oppressed, and the belly suffering pain, there is no benefit in having all other matters in perfection... TALE IX. p. 224.

۱۲. درویشی را ضرورتی پیش آمد.
کسی گفت: فلان نعمتی دارد بی قیاس، اگر بر حاجت تو واقف گردد همانا که در قضای آن توقف روا ندارد.

گفت: من او را ندانم.
گفت: منت رهبری کنم.
دستش گرفت تا به منزل آن شخص در آورد.
یکی را دید لب فرو هشته و تند نشسته.
برگشت و سخن نگفت.
کسی گفتش: چه کردی؟
گفت: عطای او را به لقای او بخشیدم.

12. A DURWAISH having a pressing want, somebody said to him, "Such an one has inconceivable wealth, and were he apprised of your condition, he would not suffer any delay to happen in supplying you."... TALE XIII. p. 227.

۱٤. حاتم طایی را گفتند: از تو بزرگ همت تر در جهان دیده‌ای یا شنیده‌ای؟ گفت: بلی! روزی چهل شتر قربان کرده بودم امرای عرب را، پس به گوشهٔ صحرایی به حاجتی برون رفته بودم، خارکنی را دیدم پشته فراهم آورده.

14. THEY asked Hatim Tai, if he had everseen or heard of any person in the world more noble-minded than himself... TALE XV. p. 229.

۱۷. یکی از عرب در بیابانی از غایت تشنگی می‌گفت:
یا لیتَ قبلَ مَنیَّتی یوماً أفوزُ بمُنیتی/ نَهراً تلاطَمُ رُکبَتی و أَظَلُّ املاءُ قِربَتی

17. AN Arab laboring under excessive thirst, exclaimed, "I wish that for one day before my death this my desire may be gratified,—that a river dashing its waves against my knees, I may fill my leather sack with water."... TALE XVIII. p. 232.

Overall, one can say that in this chapter unknown evidentials, heard, quotation, and visual evidentials are used respectively in terms of frequency of occurrence.

CHAPTER 4 OF *GOLESTĀN*

The fourth chapter of *Golestān*, called "Of the Advantages of Taciturnity," contains 14 stories (see Table 3.16).

Table 3.16 Frequency of evidentials in fourth chapter of *Golestān*

Chapter	Episodes without evidentials		Episodes with evidentials			
	Advice	Unknown source	Direct visual evidence	Heard	Quotation	Inferred/ assumed
4 Number of cases	–	8	1	3	–	2

In ten stories of this chapter you will see that there is **no known evidential**. These stories include the stories specified by the exact number:

٣. جوانی خردمند از فنون فضایل حظی وافر داشت و طبعی نافر. چندان که در محافل دانشمندان نشستی زبان سخن ببستی. باری پدرش گفت: ای پسر! تو نیز آنچه دانی بگوی. گفت: ترسم که بپرسند از آنچه ندانم و شرمساری برم.

3. A SENSIBLE young man, who had made considerable progress in learning and virtue, was at the same time so discreet, that he would sit in the company of learned men without uttering a word. Once his father said to him, "My son, why do you not also say something of what you know?": He replied: "I fear lest they should question me about something of... TALE III. p. 257.

٤. عالمی معتبر را مناظره افتاد با یکی از ملاحده لَعنهُم الله عَلی حِدَه و به حجت با او بس نیامد. سپر بینداخت و برگشت. کسی گفتش: تو را با چندین فضل و ادب که داری با بی دینی حجت نماند؟ گفت: علم من قرآن است و حدیث و گفتار مشایخ و او بدینها معتقد نیست و نمی‌شنود. مرا شنیدن کفر او به چه کار می‌آید.

4. A MAN famous for his learning, happened to have a dispute with an infidel, and finding that argument had no effect, he gave up the contest, and retired. Somebody said, "How happens it that you, who possess so much superiority in learning, virtue, and wisdom, are not a match for this infidel?"... TALE IV. p. 258.

٦. سحبان وائل را در فصاحت بی نظیر نهاده‌اند به حکم آن که بر سر جمع سالی سخن گفتی لفظی مکرّر نکردی، وگر همان اتفاق افتادی به عبارتی دیگر بگفتی. وز جمله آداب ندماء ملوک یکی این است.

6. SUHBAN Wahil has been considered as unrivalled in eloquence, insomuch that, if he spoke before an assembly for the space of a year, he did not repeat the same word twice, and if the same meaning recurred, he expressed it in a different form; and this is one of the qualifications for a courtier... TALE VI. p. 259.

۱۰. یکی از شعرا پیش امیر دزدان رفت و ثنایی بر او بگفت. فرمود تا جامه از او بر کنند و از ده به در کنند. مسکین برهنه به سرما همی‌رفت. سگان در قفای وی افتادند. خواست تا سنگی بر دارد و سگان را دفع کند، در زمین یخ گرفته بود، عاجز شد. گفت: این چه حرامزاده مردمانند، سگ را گشاده‌اند و سنگ را بسته! امیر از غرفه بدید و بشنید و بخندید. گفت: ای حکیم! از من چیزی بخواه. گفت: جامه خود می‌خواهم اگر انعام فرمایی.

10. A CERTAIN poet went to the chief of a gang of robbers, and recited verses in his praise. He ordered him to be stripped of his clothes, and expelled the village... TALE X. p. 261.

۱۱. منجمی به خانه در آمد. یکی مرد بیگانه را دید با زن او به هم نشسته. دشنام و سقط گفت و فتنه و آشوب خاست. صاحبدلی که بر این واقف بود گفت: تو بر اوج فلک چه دانی چیست/که ندانی که در سرایت کیست

11. AN astrologer entered his own house, and seeing a stranger sitting in company with his wife, abused him, and used such harsh language, that a quarrel and strife ensued... TALE XI. p. 262.

۱۲. خطیبی کریه الصوت خود را خوش آواز پنداشتی، و فریاد بیهده برداشتی. گفتی نعیب غُرابَ البَین در پرده الحان اوست، یا آیت اِنَّ انکَرَ الاصوات در شأن او.

12. A PREACHER, who had a detestable voice, but thought he had a very sweet one, bawled out to no purpose. You would say the croaking of the crow of the desert was the burden of his song, and that the following verse of the Koran was intended for him: "Verily the most detestable of sounds is the braying of an ass."... TALE XII. p. 263.

۱۳. یکی در مسجد سنجار به تطوّع بانگ گفتی به ادایی که مستمعان را از او نفرت بودی. و صاحب مسجد امیری بود عادل نیک سیرت، نمی‌خواستش

که دل آزرده گردد. گفت: ای جوانمرد! این مسجد را مؤذنانند قدیم. هر یکی را پنج دینار مرتب داشته‌ام. تو را ده دینار می‌دهم تا جایی دیگر روی.

13. A CERTAIN person, who performed gratis the office of mowuzzin in the mosque of Sanjaryah, had such a voice as disgusted all who heard it... TALE XIII. p. 264.

۱٤. ناخوش آوازی به بانگ بلند قرآن همی‌خواند. صاحبدلی بر او بگذشت. گفت: تو را مشاهره چند است؟ گفت: هیچ. گفت: پس این زحمت خود چندین چرا همی‌دهی؟ گفت: از بهر خدا می‌خوانم. گفت: از بهر خدا مخوان:
گر تو قرآن بر این نمط خوانی/ ببری رونق مسلمانی

14. A MAN with a disagreeable voice was reading the Koran, aloud, when a holy man passing by asked what was his monthly stipend. He answered, "Nothing at all." He resumed, "Why then do you take so much trouble?" He replied, "I read for the sake of God." The other rejoined, "For God's sake do not read; for if you read the Koran in this manner, you will destroy the splendor of Islamism."... TALE XIV. p. 265.

In some stories the reader will encounter the **visually seen evidentials** signifying that the writer has seen the theme of the story directly. These stories are number

۱. یکی را از دوستان گفتم: امتناع سخن گفتنم به علت آن اختیار آمده است در غالب اوقات که در سخن نیک و بد اتفاق افتد و دیدهٔ دشمنان جز بر بدی نمی‌آید. گفت: دشمن آن به که نیکی نبیند.

1. I SAID to one of my friends, "I have myself determined to observe silence, because that in conversation there frequently happens both good and evil, and the eye of an enemy observes only that which is bad."... TALE I. p. 256.

۹. در عقد بیع سرایی مترّدد بودم. جهودی گفت: آخر من از کدخدایان این محلتم. وصف این خانه چنان که هست از من پرس، بخر که هیچ عیبی ندارد. گفتم: به جز آن که تو همسایه منی!

9. I WAS hesitating about concluding a bargain for a house, when a Jew said, "I am an old householder in that quarter; inquire of me the descrip-

Evidentiality in Sa'dī's masterpieces

tion of the house, and buy it, for it has no fault." I replied: "Excepting that you are one of the neighbors ..... TALE IX. p. 261.

The heard evidentials (represented by the word "Shenidam": I heard, in the book) also will be found in stories number

۷. یکی را از حکما شنیدم که می‌گفت: هرگز کسی به جهل خویش اقرار نکرده است، مگر آن کس که چون دیگری در سخن باشد، همچنان ناتمام گفته، سخن آغاز کند.

7. I HEARD a sage say, that no one confesses his own ignorance, excepting he who begins speaking whilst another is talking, and before the discourse is ended. "O wise man, a discourse hath a commencement and a conclusion. Confound not one discourse with another. A man of virtue, judgment, and prudence speaks not until there is silence." ... TALE VII. p. 260.

Quoted evidentials

۲. زرگانی را هزار دینار خسارت افتاد. پسر را گفت: نباید که این سخن با کسی در میان نهی. گفت: ای پدر! فرمان تو راست، نگویم، ولکن خواهم مرا بر فایده این مطلع گردانی که مصلحت در نهان داشتن چیست؟ گفت: تا مصیبت دو نشود: یکی نقصان مایه و دیگر شماتت همسایه.

2. A MERCHANT, having suffered a loss of a thousand dinars, said to Ins son, "You must not mention this matter to any one." ... TALE II. p. 257.

۵. جالینوس ابلهی را دید دست در گریبان دانشمندی زده و بی حرمتی می‌کرد. گفت: اگر این نادان نبودی کار وی با نادانان بدینجا نرسیدی.

5. GALEN, on seeing a blockhead lay hold of the collar of a wise man, and disgrace him, said: "If this man had been really wise, matters would not have come to this pass with the ignorant. Strife and contention will not happen between two wise men, and a wise man will not contend with a blockhead ... TALE V. p. 259.

۸. تنی چند از بندگان محمود گفتند حسن میمندی را که: سلطان امروز تو را چه گفت در فلان مصلحت؟ گفت: بر شما هم پوشیده نباشد. گفتند: آنچه با تو گوید، به امثال ما گفتن روا ندارد. گفت: به اعتماد آن که داند که نگویم، پس چرا همی‌پرسید؟

8. SOME of the servants of the Sultan Mahmood asked Husn Miemundie what the king had said to him about a certain affair... TALE VIII. p. 260.

Overall, one can say that in this chapter unknown evidentials, heard evidentials, and visual evidentials (equally well) are used respectively in terms of frequency of occurrence.

CHAPTER 5 OF *GOLESTĀN*

The fifth chapter of *Golestān*, called "Of Love and Youth," contains 20 stories (see Table 3.17).

Table 3.17 Frequency of evidentials in fifth chapter of *Golestān*

Chapter	Episodes without evidentials		Episodes with evidentials			
	Advice	Unknown source	Direct visual evidence	Heard	Quotation	Inferred/ assumed
5 Number of cases	-	5	9	1	5	-

In some stories of this chapter you will see that there is no known evidential. These stories include the stories specified by the exact number of

٤. یکی را دل از دست رفته بود و ترک جان کرده و مطمح نظرش جایی خطرناک و مظنهٔ هلاک.
نه لقمه‌ای که مصور شدی که به کام آید یا مرغی که به دام افتد.

4. A CERTAIN person having lost his heart, abandoned himself to despair. The object of his affection being a place of danger, a whirlpool; not a morsel with which you could hope to gratify the palate; not a bird that would fall into the net... TALE IV. p. 268.

٥. یکی را از متعلمان کمال بهجتی بود و معلم از آنجا که حس بشریت است با حسن بشره او معاملتی داشت و وقتی که به خلوتش دریافتی گفتی:
نه آنچنان به تو مشغولم ای بهشتی روی/ که یاد خویشتنم در ضمیر می‌آید

5. THERE was a certain youth of most exquisite beauty, to whom his tutor, through the frailty of human nature, became so attached, that he

would be frequently recite these words: "My mind is not so weakly engaged in the contemplation of your heavenly face, that I can reserve any recollection of myself... TALE V. p. 271.

۷. یکی دوستی را که زمانها ندیده بود گفت: کجایی که مشتاق بوده‌ام؟ گفت: مشتاقی به که ملولی.

7. A PERSON who had not seen his friend for a long time said, "Where have you been whilst I was so anxious to hear of you?' He answered: "It is better to desire than to loathe... TALE VII. p. 272.

۱٤. یکی را زنی صاحب جمال جوان درگذشت و مادرزن فرتوت به علت کابین در خانه متمکن بماند و مرد از محاورت او به جان رنجیدی و از مجاورت او چاره ندیدی تا گروهی آشنایان به پرسیدن آمدندش.

14. A PERSON having a handsome wife who died, her mother, a decrepit old woman, for the sake of the dower, settled in his house... TALE XV. p. 281.

۱۸. یکی را از ملوک عرب حدیث مجنون لیلی و شورش حال او بگفتند که با کمال فضل و بلاغت سر در بیابان نهاده است و زمام عقل از دست داده. بفرمودش تا حاضر آوردند و ملامت کردن گرفت که: در شرف نفس انسان چه خلل دیدی که خوی بهایم گرفتی و ترک عشرت مردم گفتی؟

18. THEY related to one of the kings of Arabia the story of Leila and Mujnoon, and the nature of his insanity, that, whilst endowed with eminent virtues, and possessing uncommon powers of eloquence, he had abandoned himself to distraction, and retired into the desert... TALE XIX. p. 288.

In some stories, the reader will encounter the visual evidentials signifying that the writer **has seen the theme of the story directly**. These stories are number

۳. پارسایی را دیدم به محبت شخصی گرفتار نه طاقت صبر و نه یارای گفتار. چندان که ملامت دیدی و غرامت کشیدی ترک تصابی نگفتی و گفتی: کوته نکنم ز دامنت دست/ ور خود بزنی به تیغ تیزم

3. I SAW a religious man so captivated by the beauty of a youth, that his secret became public, insomuch that he suffered reproach and uneasi-

ness; however, he did not relinquish his attachment; and said, "I will not quit the skirt of your garment, although yourself should smite . . . TALE III. p. 267.

۶. شبی یاد دارم که یاری عزیز از در در آمد. چنان بیخود از جای بر جستم که چراغم به آستین کشته شد.
سَرىٰ طَيفُ مَن يَجلو بِطَلعَتِهِ الدُّجىٰ/ شگفت آمد از بختم که این دولت از کجا

6. I REMEMBER that one night one of my dearest friends entered the door, when I was so impatient to receive him, that in rising from my seat the lamp was extinguished by the sleeve of my garment . . . TALE VI. p. 272.

۸. یاد دارم در ایام پیشین که من و دوستی چون دو بادام مغز در پوستی صحبت داشتیم. ناگاه اتفاق مغیب افتاد.
پس از مدتی که باز آمد عتاب آغاز کرد که: در این مدت قاصدی نفرستادی.

8. I REMEMBER that in former times I associated so continually with a friend, that we were like a double almond. A journey unexpectedly happened . . . TALE VIII. p. 273.

۹. دانشمندی را دیدم به کسی مبتلا شده و رازش برملا افتاده. جور فراوان بردی و تحمل بی کران کردی.
باری به لطافتش گفتم: دانم که تو را در مودت این منظور علتی و بنای محبت بر زلتی نیست، با وجود چنین معنی لایق قدر علما نباشد خود را متهم گردانیدن و جور بی ادبان بردن.

9. I SAW a learned man captivated by the attachment for a person, and submitting with incredible patience to his insolent behavior. Once by way of admonition I said to him, I know that there is nothing criminal in your attachment to this person, and that this friendship is founded on pure virtue; . . . TALE IX. p. 274.

۱۰. در عنفوان جوانی چنان که افتد و دانی با شاهدی سری و سرّی داشتم به حکم آن که حلقی داشت طیّبُ الأدا وَ خَلقی کالبدرِ اذا بَدا.
آن که نبات عارضش آب حیات می‌خورد/ در شکرش نگه کند هر که نبات می‌خورد

10. IN the season of my youth it happened, as you know, that I formed a strict intimacy with a handsome youth, because he had a melodious voice, and a form beautiful as the full moon just appearing above the horizon...TALE X. p. 275.

۱۳. رفیقی داشتم که سالها با هم سفر کرده بودیم و نمک خورده و بی کران حقوق صحبت ثابت شده. آخر به سبب نفعی اندک، آزار خاطر من روا داشت و دوستی سپری شد و با این همه از هر دو طرف دلبستگی بود که شنیدم روزی دو بیت از سخنان من در مجمعی همی‌گفتند:
نگار من چو در آید به خنده نمکین/ نمک زیاده کند بر جراحت ریشان

13. I HAD a friend with whom I travelled many years; we ate our bread and salt together, and enjoyed the rights of friendship to an uncommon degree...TALE XIV. p. 280.

۱۵. یاد دارم که در ایام جوانی گذر داشتم به کویی و نظر با رویی، در تموزی که حرورش دهان بخوشانیدی و سمومش مغز استخوان بجوشانیدی.

15. I RECOLLECT that in my youth, as I was passing through a street, I cast my eyes on a beautiful girl...TALE XVI. p. 282.

۱٦. سالی محمد خوارزمشاه رحمة الله علیه با ختا برای مصلحتی صلح اختیار کرد. به جامع کاشغر در آمدم، پسری دیدم نحوی به غایت اعتدال و نهایت جمال چنان که در امثال او گویند:
معلمت همه شوخی و دلبری آموخت/ جفا و ناز و عتاب و ستمگری آموخت

16. IN the same year that Sultan Mohammed Khovaruzm Shall, for some weighty reason, made peace with the king of Khatai, I entered the mosque of Cashghur, where I saw a boy of incomparable beauty, and remarkably elegant in his form, such as those who have been thus described...TALE XVII. p. 283.

۱۷. خرقه پوشی در کاروان حجاز همراه ما بود، یکی از امرای عرب مر او را صد دینار بخشیده تا قربان کند. دزدان خفاجه ناگاه بر کاروان زدند و پاک ببردند. بازرگانان گریه و زاری کردن گرفتند و فریاد بی فایده خواندن

17. A DURWAISH accompanied me in the caravan to Mecca, on whom one of the nobles of Arabia had bestowed a hundred dinars for the support of his family ... TALE XVIII. p. 286.

The **heard evidentials** also will be found in stories number

۲۰. جوانی پاکباز پاکرو بود/ که با پاکیزه رویی در کرو بود
چنین خواندم که در دریای اعظم/ به گردابی درافتادند با هم

20. THERE was an affectionate and amiable youth who was betrothed to a beautiful girl. <u>I have heard that</u> as they were sailing on the ocean, they fell together into a whirlpool ... TALE XXI. p. 296.

Quoted evidentials

۱. حسن میمندی را گفتند: سلطان محمود چندین بندۀ صاحب جمال دارد که هر یکی بدیع جهانی‌اند. چگونه افتاده است که با هیچ یک از ایشان میل و محبتی ندارد چنان که با ایاز که حسنی زیادتی ندارد؟ گفت: هر چه به دل فرو آید در دیده نکو نماید.

1. THEY asked Husn Miemundee, "How happens it that Sultan Mahmood, having such a number of the handsome slaves, remarkable for their exquisite beauty, has not such regard and affection for any one of them as for Iyaz, who has nothing extraordinary in his appearance? ..... TALE I. p. 266.

۲. گویند خواجه‌ای را بنده‌ای نادرالحسن بود و با وی به سبیل مودت و دیانت نظری داشت.
با یکی از دوستان گفت: دریغ این بنده با حسن و شمایلی که دارد اگر زبان درازی و بی ادبی نکردی.

2. THEY tell of a certain great man, who, having a very beautiful slave, for whom he entertained a virtuous affection, said to one of his friends, "What a pity it is that this slave, who is handsome, should be rude and insolent." ... TALE II. p. 267.

۱۱. یکی را پرسیدند از مستعربان بغداد: ما تَقولُ فی المُرِدِ؟
گفت: لا خَیرَ فیهِمْ مادامَ اَحَدُهُمْ لطیفاً یَتَخاشَنُ فاذا خَشُنَ یَتَلاطَفُ. یعنی چندان که خوب و لطیف و نازک‌اندام است درشتی کند و سختی، چون سخت و درشت شد چنان که به کاری نیاید تلطف کند و درشتی نماند.

11. THEY asked one of the inhabitants of Baghdad his opinion of handsome youths. He replied: "No good is to be found amongst them, as long as they appear delicate; for then they are insolent; but when they become rough,... TALE XI. p. 277.

۱۲. یکی را از علما پرسیدند که: یکی با ماهرویییست در خلوت نشسته و درها بسته و رقیبان خفته و نفس طالب و شهوت غالب، چنان که عرب گوید التَّمرُ یانِعٌ وَ النّاطورُ غَیرُ مانِع. هیچ باشد که به قوت پرهیزگاری از او به سلامت بماند؟ گفت: اگر از مهرویان به سلامت بماند از بدگویان نماند.

12. THEY shut up a crow in the same cage with a parrot, who, distressed at the other's ugly appearance, was saying: "What is this detestable countenance, this odious form, this cursed object with unpolished manners?" TALE XIII. p. 279.

۱۹. قاضی همدان را حکایت کنند که با نعلبند پسری سر خوش بود و نعل دلش در آتش. روزگاری در طلبش متلهف بود و پویان و مترصد و جویان و برحسب واقعه گویان:
در چشم من آمد آن سهی سرو بلند/ بربود دلم ز دست و در پای فکند

19. THEY tell a story of a Cazy of Hamadan, that he was enamored with a farrier's beautiful daughter to such a degree, that his heart was inflamed by his passion like a horseshoe red hot in a forge... TALE XX. p. 290.

Overall, one can say that in this chapter visual evidentials, unknown evidentials, and then heard evidentials are used respectively in terms of frequency of occurrence.

CHAPTER 6 OF *GOLESTĀN*

The sixth chapter of *Golestān*, called "On Imbecility and Old Age," contains nine stories (see Table 3.18).

Table 3.18 Frequency of evidentials in sixth chapter of *Golestān*

Chapter	Episodes without evidentials		Episodes with evidentials			
	Advice	Unknown source	Direct visual evidence	Heard	Quotation	Inferred/ assumed
6 Number of cases	–	1	5	1	2	–

No known evidential: These stories include the stories specified by the exact number of

7. A RICH miser having a son that was sick, his friends represented that he ought either to cause the Koran to be read from beginning to end, or else offer sacrifice, that the hioji God might restore his son to health . . . TALE VII. p. 304.

In some stories, the reader will encounter the visual evidentials signifying that the writer has seen the theme of the story directly. These stories are number

١. با طایفه دانشمندان در جامع دمشق بحثی همی‌کردم که جوانی در آمد و گفت: در این میان کسی هست که زبان پارسی بداند؟ غالب اشارت به من کردند. گفتمش: خیر است!

1. I WAS engaged in a disputation with some learned men in the Mosque of Damascus, when suddenly a young man entering the gate said, "Is there any one amongst you who understands the Persian language?" . . . TALE I. p. 297.

٣. مهمان پیری شدم در دیاربکر که مال فراوان داشت و فرزندی خوبروی. شبی حکایت کرد: مرا به عمر خویش به جز این فرزند نبوده است. درختی در این وادی زیارتگاه است که مردمان به حاجت خواستن آنجا روند. شب‌های دراز در آن پای درخت بر حق بنالیده‌ام تا مرا این فرزند بخشیده است.

3. IN the territory of Diarbekr, I was the guest of a very rich old man, who had a handsome son. One night he said: "During my whole life I never had any child but this son. Near this place is a sacred tree, to which men resort to offer up their petitions. Many nights at the foot of this tree I besought God, until he bestowed on me this son." . . . TALE III. p. 301.

٤. روزی به غرور جوانی سخت رانده بودم و شبانگاه به پای گریوه‌ای سست مانده.
پیرمردی ضعیف از پس کاروان همی‌آمد و گفت: چه نشینی که نه جای خفتن است؟
گفتم: چون روم که نه پای رفتن است؟!

4. ONCE in the vigor of youth I had performed a long journey, and at night, being fatigued, remained at the foot of a mountain . . . TALE IV. p. 302.

۵. جوانی چیست لطیف خندان شیرین زبان در حلقه عشرت ما بود که در دلش از هیچ نوعی غم نیامدی و لب از خنده فرا هم. روزگاری برآمد که اتفاق ملاقات نیوفتاد. بعد از آن دیدمش زن خواسته و فرزندان خاسته و بیخ نشاطش بریده و گل هوس پژمریده.

5. AN active, pleasant, and merry youth, of agreeable manners, was one of our happy society; sorrow in no shape entered his breast, laughter would not suffer him to close his lips. A considerable time had passed without my happening to meet with him . . . . TALE V. p. 302.

٦. وقتی به جهل جوانی بانگ بر مادر زدم، دل آزرده به کنجی نشست و گریان همی‌گفت: مگر خردی فراموش کردی که درشتی میکنی؟

6. ONE day, through the ignorance of youth, I spoke sharply to my mother, which vexing her to the heart, she sat down in a corner and wept, saying: "Have you forgotten all the trouble that you gave me in your infancy, that you thus treat me with unkindness? . . . TALE VI. p. 303.

The heard evidentials (represented by the word "Shenidam": I heard, in the book) also will be found in stories number

۹. شنیده‌ام که در این روزها کهن پیری/ خیال بست به پیرانه سر که گیرد جفت بخواست دختری خوبروی گوهر نام/ چو درج گوهرش از چشم مردمان بنهفت

9. I HAVE heard that not long ago a decrepit old man, in his dotage, took it into his head to marry; and wedded a beautiful virgin named Gem, who, like a casket of jewels, had been concealed from the sight of men . . . TALE IX. p. 305.

In this chapter there won't be found any story that can be said to be the direct or indirect quotation of a specific person or source of knowledge except for story number Quoted

۲. پیرمردی حکایت کند که دختری خواسته بود و حجره به گل آراسته و به خلوت با او نشسته و دیده و دل در او بسته و شبهای دراز نخفتی و بذله‌ها و لطیفه‌ها گفتی باشد که مؤانست پذیرد و وحشت نگیرد.

2. AN old man, telling a story about himself, said: "When I married a young virgin, I bedecked a chamber with flowers, sat with her alone, and had fixed my eyes and heart solely upon her... TALE II. p. 299.

۸. پیرمردی را گفتند: چرا زن نکنی؟ گفت: با پیرزنانم عیشی نباشد. گفتند: جوانی بخواه چو مکنت داری.
گفت: مرا که پیرم با پیرزنان الفت نیست پس او را که جوان باشد با من که پیرم چه دوستی صورت بندد؟

8. THEY asked an old man why he did not marry. He answered, "I should not like an old woman." They said, "Many a young one, since you have property." He replied, "Since I, who am an old man, should not be pleased with an old woman, how can I expect that a young one would be attached to me?"... TALE VIII. p. 305.

Overall, one can say that in this chapter visual evidentials, unknown evidentials, and then heard and direct quoted are used respectively in terms of frequency of occurrence.

CHAPTER 7 OF *GOLESTĀN*

The seventh chapter of *Golestān*, called "Of the Effects of Education," contains 20 stories (see Table 3.19).

Table 3.19 Frequency of evidentials in seventh chapter of *Golestān*

Chapter	Episodes without evidentials		Episodes with evidentials			
	Advice	Unknown source	Direct visual evidence	Heard	Quotation	Inferred/ assumed
7 Number of cases	–	8	8	1	3	–

In some stories of this chapter you will see that there is no known evidential, meaning the reader won't know how Saʻdī exactly knows the story and what his source of information is. These stories include the stories specified by the exact number of

۱. یکی را از وزرا پسری کودن بود. پیش یکی از دانشمندان فرستاد که مر این را تربیتی میکن مگر که عاقل شود. روزگاری تعلیم کردش و مؤثر نبود. پیش پدرش کس فرستاد که این عاقل نمی‌باشد و مرا دیوانه کرد.

1. A CERTAIN Vizier had a stupid son, whom he sent to a learned man, desiring him to instruct him, in hopes that his capacity might improve... TALE I. p. 306.

۳. یکی از فضلا تعلیم ملک زاده‌ای همی‌داد و ضرب بی محابا زدی و زجر بی قیاس کردی. باری پسر از بی طاقتی شکایت پیش پدر برد و جامه از تن دردمند برداشت.

3. A LEARNED man, who had the education of a king's son, beat him unmercifully, and treated him with the utmost severity... TALE III. p. 308.

۵. پارسازاده ای را نعمت بیکران از ترکه عمان به دست افتاد. فسق و فجور آغاز کرد و مبذری پیشه گرفت.

5. THE son of a religious man, who succeeded to an immense fortune by the will of his uncle, became a dissipated and debauched profligate, insomuch that he left no heinous crime unpracticed, nor was there any intoxicating drug which he had not tasted... TALE V. p. 311.

٦. فقیره درویشی حامله بود، مدّت حمل بسر آورده و مر این درویش را همه عمر فرزند نیامده بود.

10. THE wife of a Durwaish was with child, and the term of pregnancy completed. The Durwaish, who never yet had a son,... TALE X. p. 316.

۱۳. هندوی نفت اندازی همی‌آموخت. حکیمی گفت تو را که خانه نیین است، بازی نه این است.

13. AN Indian was teaching others how to make fireworks, when a wise man said to him, "This is not a fit play for you who inhabit a house made of reeds."... TALE XIII. p. 318.

۱٤. مردکی را چشم درد خاست، پیش بیطار رفت که دوا کن.

14. A LITTLE man, being struck with a pain in his eyes, went to a farrier, desiring him to apply a remedy... TALE XIV. p. 319.

۱٥. یکی را از بزرگان ائمه پسری وفات یافت. پرسیدند که بر صندوق گورش چه نویسیم؟ گفت: آیات کتاب مجید را

15. A CERTAIN great man, having lost a worthy son, they asked what inscription should be put upon his gravestone... TALE XV. p. 320.

۱۶. پارسایی بر یکی از خداوندان نعمت گذر کرد که بنده‌ای را دست و پای استوار بسته عقوبت همی‌کرد. گفت: ای پسر همچو تو مخلوقی را خدای عزّ و جلّ اسیر حکم تو گردانیده است و تو را بر وی فضیلت داده شکر نعمت باری تعالی به جای آر و چندین جفا بر وی مپسند، نباید که فردای قیامت به از تو باشد و شرمساری بری.

16. A HOLY man, passing by a rich man who, having bound a slave hand and foot, was punishing him, said: "O my son, God has made subject to thee a human creature like thyself, and has given thee the superiority over him, for which return thanks to God, and do not suffer such violence to be committed... TALE XVI. p. 320.

In some stories, the reader will encounter the **visual evidentials** signifying that the writer has seen the theme of the story directly. These stories are number

۴. معلم کُتّابی دیدم در دیار مغرب ترشروی تلخ گفتار بدخوی مردم آزار گدا طبع ناپرهیزگار که عیش مسلمانان به دیدن او تبه گشتی و خواندن قرآنش دل مردم سیه کردی.

4. I SAW a schoolmaster in Africa, who had a crabbed countenance, and a bitter tongue; he was an enemy to humanity, mean-spirited, and impetuous, so that the sight of him interrupted the pleasure of Moslems, and his reading of the Koran distracted the hearts of men... TALE IV. p. 309.

۸. اعرابیی را دیدم که پسر را همی‌گفت یا بُنَّی اِنَّک مسئولٌ یومَ القیامةِ ماذا اکتَسَبتَ و لا یُقالُ بمن انتسبتَ. یعنی تو را خواهند پرسید که عملت چیست نگویند پدرت کیست.

8. I SAW an Arab who said to his son, "O my child, in the day of resurrection they will ask you, what have you done in the world; and not from whom are you descended? That is, they will inquire about your virtue, and not about your father... TALE VIII. p. 314.

۹. در تصانیف حکما آورده‌اند که کژدم را ولادت معهود نیست چنان که دیگر حیوانات را بل احشای مادر را بخورند و شکمش را بدرند و راه صحرا گیرند و آن پوست‌ها که در خانه کژدم بینند اثر آن است.

9. IN the writings of the sages, they have related that scorpions are not produced according to the ordinary course of nature, as other animals, for that they devour the mother's entrails, and tear open her belly, and flee to the desert; and the skins which are found in the holes of scorpions give proof of this matter... TALE IX. p. 315.

۱۱. طفل بودم که بزرگی را پرسیدم از بلوغ. گفت در مسطور آمده است که سه نشان دارد: یکی پانزده سالگی و دیگر احتلام و سیم بر آمدن موی پیش.

11. WHEN I was a boy, I was conversing with a holy man about manhood, who replied that the greatest proof of being arrived at a state of maturity, was one's being more intent on the means of pleasing the Almighty than how to gratify the passions ... TALE XI. p. 317.

۱۲. سالی نزاعی در پیادگان حجیج افتاده بود و داعی در آن سفر هم پیاده. انصاف در سر و روی هم فتادیم و داد فسوق و جدال بدادیم.

12. ON a certain year there happened a quarrel amongst the pilgrims, who were going onf oot to Mecca, and I was also of that number. They recriminated on one another, but at length we adjusted their differences... TALE XII. p. 318.

۱۷. سالی از بلخ بامیانم سفر بود و راه از حرامیان پر خطر. جوانی به بدرقه همراه من شد سپرباز چرخ انداز سلحشور بیش زور که به ده مرد توانا کمان او زه کردندی و زورآوران روی زمین پشت او بر زمین نیاوردندی ولیکن چنان که دانی متنعم بود و سایه پرورده نه جهاندیده و سفر کرده.

17. ON a certain year, I was travelling from Balk, with some people of Damascus, and the road was infested with robbers ... TALE XVII. p. 321.

۱۸. توانگرزاده‌ای را دیدم بر سر گور پدر نشسته و با درویش بچه‌ای مناظره در پیوسته که: صندوق تربت ما سنگین است و کتابه رنگین و فرش رخام انداخته و خشت پیروزه در او به کار برده.

18. ON a certain year, I was travelling from Balk, with some people of Damascus, and the road was infested with robbers. There was a young

man of our party, an expert handler of the shield, a mighty archer, a brandisher of all . . . TALE XVII. p. 321.

۲۰. یکی در صورت درویشان نه بر صفت ایشان در محفلی دیدم نشسته و شنعتی در پیوسته و دفتر شکایتی باز کرده و ذم توانگران آغاز کرده. سخن بدینجا رسانیده که درویش را دست قدرت بسته است و توانگر را پای ارادت شکسته.

20. I SAW, sitting in a company, a certain person who wore the habit of a Durwaish, but without possessing the disposition of one . . . TALE XX. p. 325.

The **heard evidentials** (represented by the word "Shenidam": I heard, in the book) also will be found in stories number

۷. یکی را شنیدم از پیران مربی که مریدی را همی‌گفت: ای پسر! چندان که تعلق خاطر آدمیزاد به روزیست اگر به روزیده بودی به مقام از ملائکه در گذشتی.

7. I have heard that a learned old man was saying to one of his scholar's, "If a man would but fix his mind as much on God as he does on worldly goods, he would surpass the angels . . . TALE VII. p. 314.

Quoted

۲. حکیمی پسران را پند همی‌داد که جانان پدر هنر آموزید که ملک و دولت دنیا اعتماد را نشاید و سیم و زر در سفر بر محل خطر است یا دزد به یکبار ببرد یا خواجه به تفاریق بخورد.

2. A PHILOSOPHER was thus exhorting his sons: "My dear children, acquire knowledge, for on worldly riches and possessions no reliance can be placed: rank will be of no use out of your own country, and on a journey, money is in danger of being lost; for either the thief may carry it off all at once, or the possessor may consume it by degrees . . . . TALE II. p. 307.

٦. پادشاهی پسری را به ادیبی داد و گفت: این فرزند توست، تربیتش همچنان کن که یکی از فرزندان خویش.

6. A KING placed his son with a preceptor, and said, "This is your son; educate him in the same manner as one of your own." ... TALE VI. p. 313.

۱۹. زرگی را پرسیدم در معنی این حدیث که اَعدی عدوّک نَفسُک الَّتی بینَ جَنبَیکَ.
گفت: به حکم آن که هر آن دشمنی را که با وی احسان کنی دوست گردد مگر نفس را که چندان که مدارا بیش کنی مخالفت زیادت کند.

19. THEY inquired of a religious man the meaning of this tradition,— "You have not any enemy so powerful as the passion of lust, which is within you." He replied: "Because that any enemy to whom you show kindness becomes your friend, excepting lust, the indulgence of which increases its enmity." ... TALE XIX. p. 324.

Overall, one can say that in this chapter unknown evidentials, visual evidentials and then heard and direct quoted are used respectively in terms of frequency of occurrence.

CHAPTER 8 OF *GOLESTĀN*

The last chapter of *Golestān*, called "Rules for Conduct in Life," contains 125 episodes including both poems and prose (see Table 3.20).

Table 3.20 Frequency of evidentials in eighth chapter of *Golestān*

Chapter	Episodes without evidentials		Episodes with evidentials			
	Advice	Unknown source	Direct visual evidence	Heard	Quotation	Inferred/ assumed
8 Number of cases	120	–	–	–	5	–

In four stories of this chapter you will see that there is no known evidential, meaning the reader won't know how Sa'dī exactly knows the story and what his source of information is. These stories include the stories specified by the exact number

Advice

۱. مال از بهر آسایش عمر است نه عمر از بهر گرد کردن مال. عاقلی را پرسیدند: نیکبخت کیست و بدبختی چیست؟ گفت: نیکبخت آن که خورد و کشت و بدبخت آن که مرد و هشت.

1. RICHES are for the comfort of life, and not life for the accumulation of riches ... No. I. p. 336.

۳. دو کس رنج بیهوده بردند و سعی بی فایده کردند: یکی آن که اندوخت و نخورد و دیگر آن که آموخت و نکرد.

3. Two persons took trouble in vain, and used fruitless endeavors,—he who acquired wealth, without enjoying it, and he who taught wisdom, but did not practice it ... No. III. p. 337.

Overall, one can say that in this chapter unknown evidentials, heard and visual evidentials (equally well) are used respectively in terms of frequency of occurrence.

٤. علم از بهر دین پروردن است نه از بهر دنیا خوردن.

4. Science is to be used for the preservation of religion, and not for the acquisition of wealth ... No. IV. p. 338.

٥. عالم ناپرهیزگار کور مشعله‌دار است.

5. A learned man, without temperance, is a blind man carrying a link: he showeth the road to others, but doth not guide himself ... No. V. p. 338.

٦. ملک از خردمندان جمال گیرد و دین از پرهیزگاران کمال یابد. پادشاهان به صحبت خردمندان از آن محتاج‌ترند که خردمندان به قربت پادشاهان.

6. A kingdom gains credit from wise men, and religion obtains perfection from the virtuous. Kings stand in more need of wise men than wise men do of appointments at court ... No. VI. p. 338.

۷. سه چیز پایدار نماند: مال بی تجارت و علم بی بحث و ملک بی سیاست.

7. Three things are not permanent without three things: wealth without commerce, science without argument, nor a kingdom without government... No. VII. p. 339.

٨. رحم آوردن بر بدان ستم است بر نیکان، عفو کردن از ظالمان جور است بر درویشان.

8. Showing mercy to the wicked is doing injury to the good, and pardoning oppressors is injuring the oppressed... No. VIII. p. 339.

٩. به دوستی پادشاهان اعتماد نتوان کرد و بر آواز خوش کودکان که آن به خیالی مبدل شود و این به خوابی متغیر گردد.

9. You cannot rely on the friendship of kings, nor confide in the sweet voices of boys;... No. IX. p. 339.

١٠. هر آن سری که در سر داری با دوست در میان منه چه دانی که وقتی دشمن گردد و هر گزندی که توانی، به دشمن مرسان که باشد که وقتی دوست شود.

10. Reveal not to a friend every secret that you... No. X. p. 339.

١١. دشمنی ضعیف که در طاعت آید و دوستی نماید، مقصود وی جز آن نیست که دشمنی قوی گردد.

11. A weak enemy, who becomes obedient and shows friendship, does so with no other design but to become a more powerful adversary;... No. XI. p. 340.

١٢. سخن میان دو دشمن چنان گوی که گر دوست گردند شرم زده نشوی.

12. Speak in such manner between two enemies, that, should they afterwards become friends, you may not be put to the blush... No. XII. p. 141.

١٣. هر که با دشمنان صلح می‌کند سر آزار دوستان دارد.

13. Whosoever formeth an intimacy with the enemies of his friends, does so to injure the latter. O wise man!... No. XIII. p. 341.

١٤. چون در امضای کاری مردد باشی آن طرف اختیار کن که بی آزارتر بر آید.

14. When, in transacting business, you are under any hesitation, make choice of that side which will produce the least injury ... No. XIV. p. 341.

۱۵. تا کار به زر برمی‌آید جان در خطر افکندن نشاید. عرب گوید: آخِرُ الحِیَلِ السَّیفُ چو دست از همه حیلتی در گسست / حلال است بردن به شمشیر دست

15. As long as an affair can be compassed by money, it is not advisable to put one's life in danger. When the hand has failed in every trick, it is lawful to draw the sword ... No. XV. p. 342.

۱۶. بر عجز دشمن رحمت مکن که اگر قادر شود بر تو نبخشاید.

16. Show not mercy to a weak enemy, for if he becomes powerful he will not spare you ... No. XVI. p. 342.

۱۷. نصیحت از دشمن پذیرفتن خطاست ولیکن شنیدن رواست تا به خلاف آن کار کنی که آن عین صواب است.

17. It is not advisable to follow the advice of an enemy, you may hear what he has to say, in order that you may act contrary thereto; and which is perfect reason ... No. XVII. p. 342.

۱۸. خشم بیش از حد گرفتن وحشت آرد و لطف بی وقت هیبت ببرد. نه چندان درشتی کن که از تو سیر گردند و نه چندان نرمی که بر تو دلیر شوند.

18. Anger, when excessive, createth terror; and kindness out of season destroys authority ... No. XVIII. p. 343.

۱۹. دو کس دشمن ملک و دینند: پادشاه بی حلم و زاهد بی علم.

19. Two persons are enemies to a kingdom and to religion, a monarch without clemency, and a religious man without knowledge. May there never be at the head of a kingdom a ruler who is not an obedient servant of God. No. XIX. p. 343.

۲۰. پادشه باید که تا به حدی خشم بر دشمنان نراند که دوستان را اعتماد نماند. آتش خشم اول در خداوند خشم اوفتد پس آنگه زبانه به خصم رسد یا نرسد.

20. It behooveth a king not to show wrath towards his enemies to such a degree as to alarm his friends; for the fire of wrath first falls on the exciter of it, and then the flame may reach the enemy, or not ... No. XX. p. 344.

۲۱. بدخوی در دستِ دشمنی گرفتار است که هر کجا رود از چنگِ عقوبتِ او خلاص نیابد

21. A wicked man is a captive in the hand of the enemy, for wherever he goeth he Cannot escape from the clutches of his own punishment ... No. XXI. p. 344.

Other stories containing advices are 22, 23, 24, 25 ....

Unknown evidentials

Quoted evidentials

۲. موسی، عَلَیهِ السَّلام، قارون را نصیحت کرد که: اَحْسِن کَما اَحسَنَ اللهُ الیک. نشنید و عاقبتش شنیدی.

2. The prophet Moses, upon whom be peace! thus admonished Karoon: "Do thou good, in the same manner that God hath done good unto thee." He did not listen, and you have heard of his end ... No. II. p. 336.

۲۲. جوانی با پدر گفت: ای خردمند/ مرا تعلیم ده پیرانه یک پند
بگفتا: نیکمردی کن نه چندان/ که گردد خیره گرگ تیز دندان

22. A young man said his father: "you wise man, Please advise me" He said: "be good to the others . . . ." No. XVIII. p. 343.

۱۱۸. درویشی به مناجات در میگفت: یا رب بر بدان رحمت کن که بر نیکان خود رحمت کردهای که مر ایشان را نیک آفریدهای.

118. A Durwaish, in his prayer, said, "O God, show pity towards the wicked, for on the good thou hast already bestowed mercy, by having created them virtuous." No. XCVIII. p. 374.

۱۲٤. حکیمی را پرسیدند: چندین درخت نامور که خدای عز و جل آفریده است و برومند، هیچ یک را آزاد نخواندهاند مگر سرو را که ثمرهای ندارد، در این چه حکمت است؟
گفت : هر درختی را ثمرهای معین است که به وقتی معلوم به وجود آن تازه آید و گاهی به عدم آن پژمرده شود و سرو را هیچ از این نیست و همه وقتی خوش است و این است صفت آزادگان.
بر آنچه می گذرد دل منه که دجله بسی / پس از خلیفه بخواهد گذشت در بغداد
گرت ز دست بر آید چو نخل باش کریم / ورت ز دست نیاید چو سرو باش آزاد

124. They asked a wise man, why out of many famous trees which the Almighty hath created, lofty and fruit-bearing, the cypress alone is

called free, although it beareth not fruit? He replied, "Every tree hath its appointed fruit and season, with which it is at one time flourishing\ and at another time, destitute and withering: to neither of which states the cypress is exposed, being always flourishing, as is the state of those who are free. Place not your heart on that which is transitory; for the river Tigris will continue to flow through Baghdad after that the Khalifs shall have ceased to reign. If you are able, imitate the date-tree in liberality; but if you have not the means of munificence, be free like the cypress." . . . No. CV. p. 377.

۱۰٤. در انجیل آمده است که ای فرزند آدم! گر توانگری دهمت، مشتغل شوی به مال از من و گر درویش کنمت، تنگدل نشینی. پس حلاوت ذکر من کجا دریابی و به عبادت من کی شتابی؟
گه اندر نعمتی مغرور و غافل / گه اندر تنگدستی خسته و ریش
چو در سرا و ضرّا حالت این است / ندانم کی به حق پردازی از خویش

104. It is said in the Gospel, "O sons of Adam, if I should grant you riches, you would be more intent on them than on me; and if I should make you poor, your hearts would be sorrowful; and then, how could you properly celebrate my praise, and after what manner would you worship me? Sometimes in affluence you are proud and negligent; and again in poverty, you are afflicted and wounded. Since such is your disposition, both in happiness and in misery, I know not at what time you will find leisure to worship God." . . . No. LXXXVII. p. 370.

SUMMARY AND CONCLUSIONS

Overall, one can say that in this chapter advice and unknown evidentials are used respectively much more than any kind of evidentials in terms of frequency of occurrence.

The overall results of the analysis show some facts about *Golestān* (Table 3.21):

Table 3.21 The overall results of evidentiality frequency in *Golestān*

Chapters	Episodes without evidentials		Episodes with evidentials			
	Advice	Unknown source	Direct visual evidence	Heard	Quotation	Inferred/assumed
Total number	120	76	50	20	39	–

Evidentiality in Sa'dī's masterpieces   135

1. Despite the style common in *Būstān*, Saʻdī doesn't use advice in *Golestān* except for the last chapter, which is on a topic principally needing advice.
2. Here, again, we encounter the high number of episodes without known and specific evidentials, which is much more than the ones bearing any kind of evidentials, so that in most narratives the narrator doesn't give us a hint or clue of the source of information.
3. Here, the application of direct visual evidentials is much more than the heard one, representing that Saʻdī has seen and experienced the theme of the stories much more directly than what was explained in *Būstān*.
4. The use of direct reported speech is much more than the indirect one, so that it can certainly be said that there is no indirect speech in the writing style of *Golestān*.

The result is shown in Table 3.22.

Table 3.22 Frequency of evidentials in *Golestān*

Chapters	Episodes without evidentials		Episodes with evidentials			
	Advice	Unknown source	Direct visual evidence	Heard	Quotation	Inferred/ assumed
1 Number of cases	–	21	6	9	5	–
2 Number of cases	–	21	15	1	10	–
3 Number of cases	–	12	5	6	6	–
4 Number of cases	–	8	2	1	3	–
5 Number of cases	–	5	9	1	5	–
6 Number of cases	–	1	5	1	2	–
7 Number of cases	–	8	8	1	3	–
8 Number of cases	120	4	–	–	5	–
Total number	120	76	50	20	39	–

CONCLUDING REMARKS

As the analysis of data gathered from two of Saʻdī's masterpieces shows, he prefers using advice and narrations without a specific known evidential or information source. Letting alone the advice poems or prose, the number of narrations and stories in which the unknown evidentials are used is much more than the stories containing evidentiality. This is common in both the masterpieces. But what is noticeable is the overuse of direct visual evidentiality in *Golestān* rather than *Būstān*. Another significant stylistic characteristic is Sa'dī's preference for the use of direct speech in both of the literary works. By using this linguistic mechanism, the author wants not to take the responsibility of the others' speeches. By the use of this linguistic strategy he doesn't take but shifts the responsibility to the original (reporter) speaker. Using this style, the author has obeyed the common tendency of using reported evidentials for narrating tales, besides being precise in narrating.

As the data showed, the application of inferred and assumed evidentials is rare. This shows that Sa'dī's realistic viewpoint relies on just heard and seen experiences more than assumptions and inferences.

As there is a famous saying that Sa'dī drew the picture of a real world in *Golestān* and an ideational isolated world in *Būstān*, the analysis of literary language and the linguistic mechanism will verify this famous motto and will confirm the truth of which.

3.3 Sonnets (Sa'dī, 2002/1382)

Here, in this section, the verses in which evidential markers of any kind have been used are listed based on the type of evidential (whether direct or indirect), and the total frequency number of each evidential has been offered. As most of the sonnets are ones in which there cannot be found any evidential markers (492 sonnets out of the total number of 637 sonnets listed in the *Sonnets* book) we will list just the verses in which there can be found any kind of evidentials. The numbers in parentheses show the exact number of the sonnet in which the given verse has been used.

VERSES CONTAINING EVIDENTIALS

Verses containing direct <u>visual evidentials</u>

لیکن آن نقش که در روی تو من می بینم
همه را دیده نباشد که ببینند آن را

1. But that image which <u>I see</u> in your face
   Can not be seen by all the people

$$\text{لبت بدیدم و لعلم بیوفتاد از چشم}$$
$$\text{سخن بگفتی و قیمت برفت لؤلؤ را}$$

2. I <u>saw</u> your lips and I cried
   starting speaking, the pearls lost its cost and value

$$\text{من بدین خوبی و زیبایی ندیدم روی را}$$
$$\text{وین دلاویزی و دلبندی نباشد موی را}$$

3. I <u>haven't seen</u> any face as beautiful as yours
   Nor any beautiful hair, more beautiful than yours

$$\text{مرا به شاعری آموخت روزگار آن گه}$$
$$\text{که چشم مست تو دیدم که ساحری آموخت}$$

4. The fate made me a poet
   Upon <u>seeing</u> your eyes that taught me magic powers

$$\text{من هم اول که دیدمت گفتم}$$
$$\text{حذر از چشم مست خون خوارت}$$

5. From the first moment that I <u>saw</u> you I told that
   I shall run away from your bloodthirsty eyes

$$\text{هر آدمي که چنین شخص دلستان بیند}$$
$$\text{ضرورتست که گوید به سرو ماند راست}$$

6. For everybody who <u>sees</u> such a charming one
   It is necessary to say that the one is like cypress in rigidity

$$\text{چون روی تو صورتی ندیدم}$$
$$\text{در شهر که مبطل صلات است}$$

7. I didn't <u>see</u> any face as yours
   In the city which is the cause of canceling the prayer

$$\text{بسیار دیده ایم درختان میوه دار}$$
$$\text{زین به ندیده ایم که در بوستان توست}$$

8. I <u>have seen</u> so many fruitful trees
   None of them much better than what is in your garden

از رشک آفتاب جمالت بر آسمان
هر ماه ماه دیدم چون ابروان توست

9. Out of envy of your beauty
   Every month I <u>saw</u> the moon in the sky which resembles your eyebrows

آن پری کز خلق پنهان بود چندین روزگار
باز می بینم که در عالم پدیدار آمده ست

10. That fairy who were hidden from the sight some days
    I see her again who is apparent in the world

افسوس بر آن دیده که روی تو ندیده ست
یا دیده و بعد از تو به رویی نگریده ست

11. Alas!/I feel sorry for the eyes which <u>haven't seen</u> you
    Or those which <u>have seen</u> you but <u>turned the eyes</u> to the other face

دوش آرزوی خواب خوشم بود یک زمان
امشب نظر به روی تو از خواب خوشتر ست

12. Last night I wished a sweat dream for some moment
    Tonight <u>looking at your face</u> is sweater than dream

با خردمندی و خوبی پارسا و نیکخوست
صورتی هرگز ندیدم کاین همه معنی در اوست

13. With wisdom and goodness pious and good
    <u>I've never seen</u> a face that has all this meaning in him

چون دیدمش آن رخ نگارین
در خود به غلط شدم که این اوست

14. When I <u>saw</u> her beautiful face
    I was mistaken that this is her

سرمست درآمد از درم دوست
لب خنده زنان چو غنچه در پوست

15. My friend <u>came across</u> me while drunk
    Smiling like a bud in its covering shell

Evidentiality in Sa'dī's masterpieces   139

کس به چشمم در نمی آید که گویم مثل اوست
خود به چشم عاشقان صورت نبندد مثل دوست

16. No one comes to my eyes to say that she is like her
    Don't fall into the eyes of lovers like the friend

مرا که دیده به دیدار دوست برکردم
حلال نیست که بر هم نهم به تیر از دوست

17. I who have seen the friend
    Must not turn my eyes from the arrows thrown by the friend

گفتم مگر به خواب ببینم خیال دوست
اینک علی الصباح نظر بر جمال دوست

18. I said to myself maybe I see dream of the friend in my dream
    Now I see beauty of the friend in morning

سروها دیدم در باغ و تأمل کردم
قامتی نیست که چون تو به دلارایی هست

19. I have seen the cedars in garden and meditated
    There is no stature like you cause you have a heart

همه کس را مگر این ذوق نباشد که مرا
کان چه من می نگرم بر دگری ظاهر نیست

20. Not everyone's joy like me
    Seeing what I see is not possible for others

زان گه که بر آن صورت خوبم نظر افتاد
از صورت بی طاقتیم پرده برافتاد

21. As long as I looked at that good face
    My impatient face was unveiled

به چشم دل نظرت می کنم که دیده سر
ز برق شعله دیدار در نمی گنجد

22. I see you with my heart
    My eyes can not tolerate the light of your presence

از خیال تو به هر سو که نظر می کردم
پیش چشمم در و دیوار مصور می شد

23. Whatever I saw except for your mental imagery
    In front of my eyes, there was nothing but the door and wall

مرغان چمن نعره زنان دیدم و گویان
زین غنچه که از طرف چمنزار برآمد

24. I <u>saw</u> the birds singing in the grass
    Upon seeing the bud that came out of the grassland

تا گل روی تو دیدم همه گل ها خارند
تا تو را یار گرفتم همه خلق اغیارند

25. All the others are thorns, seen <u>I saw</u> you
    They became strangers, when I chose you

کس نمی بینم ز بیرون سرای
و اندرونم مرحبایی می زند

26. I <u>don't see</u> anyone out of the home
    I am happy from my inside

تو عاشقان مسلم ندیده ای سعدی
که تیغ بر سر و سر بنده وار در پیشند

27. You <u>have not seen</u> the real love Sa'dī
    They embrace the arrows and they are purly on the way (They are ready for what will happen next)

خاک شیراز چو دیبای منقش دیدم
وان همه صورت شاهد که بر آن دیبا بود

28. I saw the soil of Shiraz like a colorful Dibā
    There were so many beautiful figures and faces on that Dibā

من باری از تو بر نتوانم گرفت چشم
گم کرده دل هرآینه در جست و جو بود

29. I can't help <u>watching</u> you
My heart will always search for you, for I have lost my heart

ره ندیدم چو برفت از نظرم صورت دوست
همچو چشمی که چراغش ز مقابل برود

30. I lost my path when I lost the friend's face
It would be like an eye that lost its sight

کس ندیدست آدمیزاد از تو شیرین تر سخن
شکر از پستان مادر خورده ای یا شیر را

31. No one has <u>seen</u> the sweetness and grace of his/her
No one will want to miss her/his glance again

گفتم از ورطه عشقت به صبوری به درآیم
باز می بینم و دریا نه پدید است کرانش

32. I said to myself that I will endure her love by patience
I <u>see</u> her again and the sea shore is not apparent

به عمر خویش ندیدم شبی که مرغ دلم
نخواند بر گل رویت چه جای بلبل باغ

33. In my lifetime I <u>have not seen</u> any night when my heart like a bird
Sings for your face which is like a flower, is there any need for nightingale?

جلوه کنان می روی و باز می آیی
سرو ندیدم بدین صفت متمایل

34. You represent yourself when you go and come
I <u>have never seen</u> any cypress so beautiful like you

گفتم چو طاووسی مگر عضوی ز عضوی خوبتر
می‌بینمت چون نیشکر شیرینی از سر تا قدم

35. I said you're always beautiful like a peafowl
<u>I see</u> you that you're sweet like sugar

نگاه می‌کنم از پیش رایت خورشید
که می‌برد به افق پرچم سپاه ظلام

36. <u>I watch</u> that before the figure of sun
    They take the flag of blackness to the horizon

مرا دو دیده به راه و دو گوش بر پیغام
تو مستریح و به افسوس می‌رود ایام

37. <u>My eyes stared</u> at roads and my ears ready to hear the message
    You are so calm and relax but my days pass so hardly

من همان روز که آن خال بدیدم گفتم
بیم آن است بدین دانه که در دام افتم

38. As I saw her/him sign I said
    Warning! I will fall into his/her trap

گفتم ببینمش مگر م درد اشتیاق
ساکن شود بدیدم و مشتاق‌تر شدم

39. I told myself when I see her/him it will lessen the pain
    I <u>saw</u> and I felt lovely about him/her again

دیدم دل خاص و عام بردی
من نیز دلاوری نمودم

40. <u>I saw</u> you gave your heart to different people
    I also tried to take your heart for myself

دو هفته می‌گذرد کان مه دو هفته ندیدم
به جان رسیدم از آن تا به خدمتش نرسیدم

41. It's been two weeks <u>I haven't seen</u> her
    I lost my patience since I didn't reach her

من چون تو به دلبری ندیدم
گلبرگ چنین طری ندیدم

42. <u>I never seen</u> someone like you
    <u>I never seen</u> so fresh petals like you

Evidentiality in Sa'dī's masterpieces

گر به رخسار چو ماهت صنما می نگرم
به حقیقت اثر لطف خدا می نگرم

43. If <u>I look</u> at you my friend
In fact <u>I look</u> at God's grace on you

امروز مبارک است فالم
کافتاد نظر بر آن جمالم

44. Today was is best day
Because <u>I looked</u> at her beauty

چشم که بر تو می‌کنم چشم حسود می‌کنم
شکر خدا که باز شد دیده بخت روشنم

45. As <u>I see</u> you I put bad eyes away from you
Thank God for giving love to me again

همه بینند نه این صنع که من می‌بینم
همه خوانند نه این نقش که من می‌خوانم

46. Everyone <u>sees</u> but not what <u>I see</u>
They all talk about it but not what I talk

سخن از نیمه بریدم که نگه کردم و دیدم
که به پایان رسدم عمر و به پایان نرسانم

47. I stopped talking and <u>I watch and I saw</u>
My life will be over and I didn't do anything

منم یا رب در این دولت که روی یار می‌بینم
فراز سرو سیمینش گلی بر بار می‌بینم

48. I'm the one who is fortunate <u>seeing</u> my love
<u>I see</u> at the top of the cypress a flower

دلم تا عشقباز آمد در او جز غم نمی‌بینم
دلی بی غم کجا جویم که در عالم نمی‌بینم

49. Since I am a lover, <u>I see</u> nothing except pain
Where to look for a heart without any pain which <u>I can't see</u> in the world

از آن ساعت که دیدم گوشوارش
ز چشمانم بیفتاده ست پروین

50. Since the hour that <u>I saw</u> her earrings
    I lost my interest in Pleiades

در همه گیتی نگاه کردم و باز آمدم
صورت کس خوب نیست پیش تصاویر او

51. <u>I looked</u> at everywhere in this universe
    no one's good in front of his/her images

چه روی است آن که دیدارش ببرد از من شکیبایی
گواهی می دهد صورت بر اخلاقش به زیبایی

52. What a face <u>visiting</u> of whom will lose my patience
    The face testifies her ethics beautifully

ندیدم آبی و خاکی بدین لطافت و پاکی
تو آب چشمه حیوان و خاک غالیه بویی

53. <u>I have never seen</u> water or soil so gentle and pure like you
    You are really water of life and aromatic soil

من آدمی به جمالت نه دیدم و نه شنیدم
اگر گلی به حقیقت عجین آب حیاتی

54. <u>I neither saw</u> or heard of any man so beautiful
    If you're created from mud you were created from water of life

ندیدمت که بکردی وفا بدان چه بگفتی
طریق وصل گشادی من آمدم تو برفتی

55. <u>I didn't see</u> you doing what you have told
    You promised to be with each other but I came and you had gone

تا من در این سرایم این در ندیده بودم
کامروز پیش چشمم در بوستان گشادی

56. As long as I am here <u>I didn't see</u> this door
    Until you came and opened this special door before my eyes

    از بس که در نظرم خوب آمدی صنما
    هر جا که می نگرم گویی که در نظری

57. As you show me yourself good enough to me
    when I look everywhere <u>I see</u> you there in my imagination

    آمدمت که بنگرم باز نظر به خود کنم
    سیر نمی شود نظر بس که لطیف منظری

58. I come here <u>to see</u> you again
    I can't stop looking at you cause you're so beautiful and gentle in face

    دیدم امروز بر زمین قمری
    همچو سروی روان به رهگذری

59. <u>I saw</u> someone today on earth
    Who was like a walking cypress passing the passengers

    حور بهشت خوانمت ماه تمام گویمت
    کآدمیی ندیده‌ام چون تو پری به دلبری

60. I define you as being like a full moon, for
    <u>I haven't seen</u> any fairy so beautiful like you in flirting

    سرو روان ندیده ام جز تو به هیچ کشوری
    هم نشنیده ام که زاد از پدری و مادری

61. <u>I haven't seen</u> any walking cypress in any country
    I haven't heard that has been born from any parents

    یار گرفته ام بسی چون تو ندیده ام کسی
    شمع چنین نیامده ست از در هیچ مجلسی

62. I have had so many friends like you, <u>I haven't seen</u> someone like you
    There has not been any candle like you in any party

چنین قیامت و قامت ندیده ام همه عمر
تو سرو یا بدنی شمس یا بناگوشی

63. <u>I have never seen</u> any like what you have in my whole life
    What exactly you are? cypress or body? Sun or parotid?

ای دریغا گر شبی در بر خرابت دیدمی
سرگران از خواب و سرمست از شرابت دیدمی

64. What a pity that <u>I saw you</u> so sorrowful beside me
    So drunk and in need of sleeping

ای که به حسن قامتت سرو ندیده ام سهی
گر همه دشمنی کنی از همه دوستان بهی

65. <u>I have never seen</u> someone attractive like you
    If you act in a bad way you are better than all friends

وجود هر که نگه می‌کنم ز جان و جسد
مرکب است و تو از فرق تا قدم جانی

66. As <u>I look</u> everyone from soul and body
    You are completely mixed and you darling are totally soul from top of the head to the toe

نظر آوردم و بردم که وجودی به تو ماند
همه اسمند و تو جسمی همه جسمند و تو جانی

67. I looked and <u>I saw</u> that there was some body like you
    All of them are names, you are the body. All are bodes and you are soul

Direct evidentials (other senses except for visuals)

ز اندازه بیرون تشنه‌ام ساقی بیار آن آب را
اول مرا سیراب کن وآنگه بده اصحاب را

1. <u>I am so thirsty</u> bring me the water
   Give me water first then give it to others

دیگر نشنیدیم چنین فتنه که برخاست
از خانه برون آمد و بازار بیاراست

2. I haven't ever heard of the crisis she made
   She came out of the house and decorated the mall

دشنام کرم کردی و گفتی و شنیدم
خرم تن سعدی که برآمد به زبانت

3. You made insult to me and I heard it
   How beautiful it was that you utterd Sa'dī's name

همچو مستسقی بر چشمه نوشین زلال
سیر نتوان شدن از دیدن مهرافزایت

4. Like a man who is so thirsty that cannot be full and he is beside a pure sweet spring
   I can't be full of your love making sight

همچنان داغ جدایی جگرم می‌سوزد
مگرم دست چو مرهم بنهی بر دل ریش

5. My liver is burning from the pain of separation
   The only way that can heal my pain in liver is that you touch my heart

یک امشبی که در آغوش شاهد شکرم
گرم چو عود بر آتش نهند غم نخورم

6. Tonight when the sweet love craddles me in her arms
   I won't sorrow if they put me on the fire like agarwood

وه که در عشق چنان می سوزم
که به یک شعله جهان می سوزم

7. I am really burning with love
   Seems I can burn the world with that flame

بوی پیراهن گم کرده خود می شنوم
گر بگویم همه گویند ضلالیست قدیم

8. I smell the smell of my lost dress
   If I say this it will be said to me that I am led astray from past times

هر کو شراب فرقت چشیده باشد
داند که سخت باشد قطع امیدواران

9. Anyone who has tasted the wine of separation
   Knows it can be hard to lose hope

رقیب انگشت می خاید که سعدی چشم بر هم نه
مترس ای باغبان از گل که می بینم نمی چینم

10. The rival is angry and frightened and he says: "Sa'dī close your eyes"
    Don't worry, the gardener! I see the flower but I don't want to pick it

INDIRECT EVIDENTIALS (HEARSAY, DIRECT SPEECH, AND INDIRECT REPORTED SPEECH)

Heard/hearsay

هرگز نشنیده‌ام که بادی
بوی گلی از تو خوشتر آورد

1. I have never heard a wind
   Brings such a pleasant smell more pleasant than yours

نشنیده ام که ماهی بر سر نهد کلاهی
یا سرو با جوانان هرگز رود به راهی

2. I haven't ever heard of any cypress which wears hat
   Or any cypress which goes with the youth in a road

شنیده ام که تو را التماس شعر رهیست
تو کان شهد و نباتی شکر چه می خواهی

3. I have heard that you beg them to compose poems for you
   You who are the source of sweetness! What else do you want (why do you want such thing)?

شنیده ام که تو را التماس شعر رهیست
تو کان شهد و نباتی شکر چه می خواهی

4. I have heard that you beg them to compose poems for you
You who are the source of sweetness! What else do you want (why do you want such thing)?

هرگز نشنیده ام که کرده ست
سرو آنچه تو می کنی به جولان

5. I haven't ever heard of what cypress
Does like what you do when walking

بر سرو قامتت گل و بادام روی و چشم
نشنیده ام که سرو چنین آورد بری

6. On your height cypress there hung flowers and almond (beautiful eye and face)
I haven't ever heard of any cypress which bears such a fruit

هرگز جماعتی که شنیدند سر عشق
نشنیده ام که باز نصیحت شنیده اند

7. Those who have heard the secret of live
I have not heard of that they ever received advices again

هرگز وجود حاضر غایب شنیده ای
من در میان جمع و دلم جای دیگر است

8. Have you ever heard a person who is present but actually absent?
I'm in crowd but my heart is somewhere else

کس مثل تو خوبروی فرزند
نشنید که هیچ مادر آورد

9. No one heard that a mother give birth
A good child like you

گویند نظر به روی خوبان
نهیست نه این نظر که ما راست

10. It is said that looking good people
    Is forbidden but not what we see

وان سرو که گویند به بالای تو باشد
هرگز به چنین قامت و رفتار نباشد

11. That cypress which is said resembles you in height
    Is never just like you in height and manner

آن سرو که گویند به بالای تو ماند
هرگز قدمی پیش تو رفتن نتواند

12. That cypress which is said is like you
    Cannot ever go one step forward across you (in no way resembles you)

Reports speech

گوید ن مگ و سعدی چندین سخن از عشقش
میگویم و بعد از من گویند به دوران ها

1. They said: " don't talk about his or her love"
   I say it and after me it will be said to the offspring

رقیب انگشت میخاید که سعدی چشم بر هم نه
مترس ای باغبان از گل که می بینم نمی چینم

2. The rival is angry and frightened and he says: "Sa'dī close your eyes"
   Don't worry, the gardener! I see the flower but I don't want to pick it

عاشقی می‌گفت و خوش خوش می‌گریست
جان بیاساید که جانان قاتل است

3. A lover was saying and crying:
   "My soul will rest, for the beloved is the killer"

آن که می گوید نظر در صورت خوبان خطاست
او همین صورت همی بیند ز معنی غافلست

4. One who says: "looking on good people faces is wrong"
   He or she sees only outside and they ignore inside

بسی بگفت خداوند عقل و نشنیدم
که دل به غمزه خوبان مده که سنگ و سبوست

5. The ration frequently said and I didn't listen:
   "Don't give heart to the great which resembles stone against a cup"

دوستان گویند سعدی دل چرا دادی به عشق
تا میان خلق کم کردی وقار خویش را

6. Friends say: "Sa'dī! tent on the garden covered with flowers"
   I love a flower that is not in a garden full of flowers

ماجرای عقل پرسیدم ز عشق
گفت معزولست و فرمانیش نیست

7. I asked ration the love story
   It said: "it is fired and it has no power and order"

(بوستان روحانی) گفت سعدی خیال خیره مبند
سیب سیمین برای چیدن نیست

8. He (bustān-e rohāni) said: "Sa'dī! don't even think about it
   Cause this is a silver apple which should not be picked up

دیده ام می جست و گفتندم نبینی روی دوست
خود درفشان بود چشمم کاندر او سیماب داشت

9. I was looking and they told me: "you won't see her face"
   I was shedding the tears and within which there was mercury

با هر که مشورت کنم از جور آن صنم
گوید ببایدت دل از این کار برگرفت

10. Whoever I consult with from the tyranny of my beloved
    Will say: "you should stop this love affair"

(عقل) گفت در راه دوست خاک مباش
نه که بر دامنش نشیند گرد

11. The ration said: "don't be like soil in front of the beloved,
    Unless there will be dust on her dress"

گویند نظر چرا نبستی
تا مشغله و خطر نباشد

12. They say: "why didn't you stop watching
    So that there would be no danger and concern"

(یار) به خنده گفت که من شمع جمعم ای سعدی
مرا از آن چه که پروانه خویشتن بکشد

13. My beloved said: "Sa'dī! I am the candle in this meeting
    It is none of my business that the butterfly kills itself"

نامم به عاشقی شد و گویند توبه کن
توبت کنون چه فایده دارد که نام شد

14. I lost my fame and it they said to me: "Repent"
    What is the use of repentance, while there remains no fame?

عیب جویانم حکایت پیش جانان گفته اند
من خود این پیدا همی گویم که پنهان گفته اند

15. Those who reproach and blame me have told the story to my beloved
    I myself will say this overtly, what have been said covertly

پیش از این گویند کز عشقت پریشانست حال
گر بگفتندی که مجموعم پریشان گفته اند

16. They said about me that I am diffused and distracted by your love
    They mistakenly said that, if they said that I am focused

سحر گویند حرامست در این عهد ولیک
چشمت آن کرد که هاروت به بابل نکند

17. It is said that magic is a sin nowadays
    Your eyes has done (to me) that Hārut has not done to Babel

    گویند چرا سعدی از عشق نپرهیزد
    من مستم از این معنی هشیار سری باید

18. They say: "why Saʿdī does not avoid such a love"
    I am drunk of this meaning. There must be a wise man to avoid the love

    گویند دوستانم سودا و ناله تا کی
    سودا ز عشق خیزد ناله ز غم برآید

19. My friends say how long do you want to continue hallucination
    Hallucination comes out of love and whine out of sorrow

    همی‌خرامد و عقلم به طبع می‌گوید
    نظر بدوز که آن بی‌نظیر می‌آید

20. She is walking pleasantly and my ration is telling me:
    "Don't look while that unique figure is coming"

    دی گفت سعدیا من از آن توام به طنز
    این عشوه دروغ دگربار بنگرید

21. Yesterday, she said: "Saʿdī! I belong to you."
    Listen to this false charm again.

    مرا گویند چشم از وی بپوشان
    ورا گو برقعی بر خویشتن پوش

22. It is said to me: "don't look at her"
    Say to her: "dress in Burqa"

    به خنده گفت که سعدی از این سخن بگریز
    کجا روم که به زندان عشق دربندم

23. She said while smiling: "skip this proposition"
    Where shall I go, for I am imprisoned in the jail of love

گویند سعدیا مکن از عشق توبه کن
مشکل توانم و نتوانم که نشکنم

24. They say: "Sa'dī! don't do this. Repent of that love"
    It is difficult for me to do that and I cannot help keeping the repentance

گویند مکن سعدی جان در سر این سودا
گر جان برود شاید من زنده به جانانم

25. They say: "Sa'dī! don't lose your life by this hallucination"
    It does worth if I lose my life. I am alive through the beloved.

گویند بدار دستش از دامن
تا دست بدارد از گریبانم

26. They say: "don't hold her skirt (meaning skip the love and let her go)
    (I shall do this) just when she doesn't hold my collar (meaning if she lets me go)

پرسید که چونی ز غم و درد جدایی
گفتم نه چنانم که توان گفت که چونم

27. Somebody asked: "how are you getting along with the pain of separation?"
    I said I am not in a status to say how I am

گفتی که چون من در زمی دیگر نباشد آدمی
ای جان لطف و مردمی ما نیز هم بد نیستیم

28. You said: "there isn't any human like me on the earth"
    You the essence of kindness and humanity! We are not too bad, too.

گفتم تو ما را دیده ای وز حال ما پرسیده ای
پس چون ز ما رنجیده ای ما نیز هم بد نیستیم

29. I said: "you have seen us, you have asked us about our status"
    Why have you been offended, We are not too bad, too.

گفتی به از من در چگل صورت نبندد آب و گل
ای سست مهر سخت دل ما نیز هم بد نیستیم

30. You said: "there isn't anybody more beautiful than me in beauty."
    Hey thee unkind cold-heart! We are not too bad, too.

گفتی ز خاک بیشترند اهل عشق من
از خاک بیشتر نه که از خاک کمتریم

31. You said: "those who are my lovers are much more than soil in number"
    We are not more than that, but less than soil

دوش می گفت که سعدی غم ما هیچ ندارد
می نداند که گرم سر برود دست نشویم

32. Last night she said: "Sa'dī does not suffer from any pain about me"
    She does not know that if I lose my head, I won't let the love go

کسان گویند چون سعدی جفا دیدی تحول کن
رها کن تا بمیرم بر سر کوی وفاداران

33. They say: "Sa'dī! while suffering, tolerate"
    You release me in order for me to die with those royalties

چرخ شنید ناله‌ام گفت منال سعدیا
کآه تو تیره می‌کند آینه جمال من

34. The world heard my sorrowful whine. It said: "Sa'dīyā! don't whine, for
    Your whine makes my mirror of beauty so unclear and blurry

با جوانان راه صحرا برگرفتم بامداد
کودکی گفتا تو پیری با خردمندان نشین

35. I went to the deserts with the youth
    A child said: "you are elderly, go and sit beside to the old ones"

بازم حفاظ دامن همت گرفت و گفت
از دوست جز به دوست مبر سعدیا پناه

36. The endeavor/effort prevented me again and it said:
    "Sa'dīyā! Don't shelter and resort from the beloved to anything except to the beloved"

گویند رفیقانم در عشق چه سر داری
گویم که سری دارم درباخته در پایی

37. My friends say to me: "what are you going to do with love"
    I say: "I am going to lose my head for that figure's head"

هر که می بینــدم از جور غمت می گوید
سعدیا بر تو چه رنج است که بگداخته ای

38. Everybody who sees me for the tyranny of your pain will say:
    "Saʿdīyā! why do you suffer so much that you have been so burnt-out"

چنین گویند سعدی را که دردی هست پنهانی
خبر در مغرب و مشرق نبودی گر نهانستی

39. They say: "There is some hidden sorrow and pain with Saʿdī"
    If that pain was hidden, there wouldn't be any news about it from east to west

گفته بودی با تو در خواهی کشید جام وصال را
جرعه ای نا خورده شمشیر جفا برداشتی

40. You had said: "I will drink the joining wine with you"
    not sipped (at) her wine, you took the spear for oppression

به خنده گفت که سعدی سخن دراز مکن
میان تهی و فراوان سخن چو طنبوری

41. She said while smiling: "don't speak so much
    You are so talkative and so void of meaning that you resemble tanbur"

سروی به لب جویی گویند چه خوش باشد
آنان که ندیدستند سروی به لب بامی

42. They say: "how beautiful is the cypress across the stream"
    Those are the ones who haven't ever seen the cypress across the top roof

سعدیا دیگر این حدیث مگوی
تا نگویند قصه می‌خوانی

43. Sa'dīyā! Don't say this story again
    So that they don't say that you are telling the story

$$گفتی که دیر و زود به حالت نظر کنم$$
$$آری کنی چو بر سر خاکم گذر کنی$$

44. You said: "I will keep a watchful eye on you sooner or later"
    Yes, you will but only when you pass my grave

$$گفتی نظر خطاست تو دل می بری رواست$$
$$خود کرده جرم و خلق گنهکار می کنی$$

45. You said: "watching me is not a right deed." Is it right that you are flirting?
    You did the crime and you accuse the people of the crime

$$دی به امید گفتمش داعی دولت توام$$
$$گفت دعا به خود بکن گر به نیاز می کنی$$

46. Yesterday, with so much hope in my heart I said to her: "I pray for you."
    She said: "Pray for yourself, if in need of."

$$روزی به زنخدانت گفتم به سیمینی$$
$$گفت ار نظری داری ما را به از این بینی$$

47. One day I told to your chin: "you are like a silver quince
    it said: "if you like me, you will see me much more better than this."

Indirect evidentials (inferred/assumed/argumentative)

$$سعدی از آنجا که فهم اوست سخن گفت$$
$$ور نه کمالِ تو، و هم کی رسد آنجا؟$$

1. Sa'dī said something according to his own understanding
   Unless imagination can't afford to understand your perfection (1)

$$گفتیم عشق را به صبوری دوا کنیم$$
$$هر روز عشق بیشتر و صبر کمتر است$$

2. We <u>assumed</u> that it is possible to treat love by patience
   Every day love gets more and more and patience gets less and less (64)

ما پراکندگان مجموعیم
یار ما غایب است و در نظر است

3. We are distracted focused
   Our beloved is absent, while she is still into sight

نپندارم که در بستان فردوس
بروید چون تو سروی بر لب جوی

4. I don't suppose that in paradise garden
   There will be a cypress like you across the stream

ندانمت ز کجا آن سپر به دست آید
که تیر آه من از آسمان بگردانی

5. I don't know from where you get the shield
   That you deviate the whine arrow in the sky

Table 3.23 Frequency of evidentials in *Sonnets*

Evidential type	Episodes without evidentials	Episodes with evidentials			
		Direct visual evidence	Other senses	Quotation	Inferred/ assumed
Total number	492	67	10	Heard/ hearsay 12	Reported speech 47	5

Reference list

Gladwin, F. (1865). *Gulistan, or Rose Garden*. Cambridge: Cambridge University Press.

Krippendoff, K. (2004/1383). *Mabani tahlil goftman[Content Analysis: An Introduction to Its Methodology]*. Translated by HoshngNayebi. Tehran: Ney Publication.

Mahlberg, M. (2016). Corpus stylistics. In V. Sotirova (ed.), *The Bloomsbury Companion to Stylistics*. London: Bloomsbury Academic An imprint of Bloomsbury Publishing.

Saʻdī, M. (2003/1382 Š). *Sonnets*. (Edited by Mohamma Ali Foroughi. 16th edition). Tehran: Ghoghnus publication.

Saʻdī, M. (2017a/1396 Š). *Būstān*. (Edited by GholāmHosseinYūsefī. 12th edition). Tehran: Khārazmī.

Saʻdī, M. (2017b/1396 Š). *Golestān*. (Edited by GholāmHosseinYūsefī. 12th edition). Tehran: Khārazmī.

4 Evidentiality in the three literary works

4.1 Cross-comparison of evidentials in the three masterpieces

As Table 4.1 shows, there is a tiny difference in the use of evidentiality as used in the three literary works that have been of our concern throughout this book.

The numbers presented Table 4.1 show the fact that in the three literary works the total number of episodes, stories, or sonnets in which there can't be found any evidential type is more than the ones containing evidentials of any type. That can be explained as the general tendency of Saʿdī as his literary style.

4.2 Peculiarities of Saʿdī's literary style in *Būstān*, *Golestān*, and *Sonnets*

As can be figured out from the numbers summarized in the Table 4.1, in *Būstān* the number of heard and hearsay evidentials are much more than the directly seen events, which leads to firsthand seen/visual evidentials. But in both *Golestān* and *Sonnets* the direct visual evidentials are much more than the heard and hearsay ones. That can be explained as the general tendency of Saʿdī to explain the real events or real beloved, which were seen by Saʿdī respectively in *Golestān* and *Sonnets*. This can show that Saʿdī in *Būstān* is trying to illustrate the ideational world as heard from the elderly or the wise men, but in *Golestān* and *Sonnets* he is trying to depict the image of what he has seen or heard.

In *Golestān* he tries to illustrate the picture of the real events and scenes he has experienced directly through his own trips and social intercourses. In *Sonnets* he tries to show his emotions (whether happiness or sadness) as his reaction to the beloved seen for the first time as an eyewitnessed scene. It is important to note that much emotional response to literature is empathic and

Table 4.1 Cross-comparison of evidentials in the masterpieces

books	Episodes without evidentials		Episodes with evidentials			
	Advice	Unknown source	Direct visual evidence	Heard	Quotation	Inferred/ assumed
1 **Būstān**	80	91	20	64	16	–
2 **Golestān**	120	76	50	20	39	–
3 **Sonnets**		492	67	12	47	5

it is evoked mainly by these attempts to make mental images. Hogan (2014: 518) believes that emotion systems involve neural circuits that are activated by *eliciting conditions*. For example, in a story, the appearance of the hero's gun-wielding nemesis may be an eliciting condition for fear. Eliciting conditions lead to a variety of *outcomes*. These fall into three broad categories:

> *physiological*, *actional*, and *expressive*. Physiological outcomes are the changes in bodily conditions that accompany the activation of an emotion. These include, for example, alterations in heart rate, respiration, perspiration, and so on. Actional outcomes are behaviors that have the purpose of altering or sustaining eliciting conditions. These are typically motor responses, but they may also be cognitive modulations. For example, the standard actional outcome when faced with fear-eliciting danger is flight. This aims to change the eliciting conditions by removing the danger. . . . Expressive outcomes are external manifestations of the activation of an emotion system, such as weeping in the case of sorrow. However, they do not serve to alter the eliciting conditions directly. Rather, they serve to communicate emotion, perhaps altering the eliciting conditions indirectly. Expressive outcomes include facial expressions, posture, gait, pupil dilation, vocalization, and so on. Emotion expressions are themselves eliciting conditions for emotions in observers. Expressive outcomes are clearly relevant to emotion in art—through, for example, the representation of emotionally expressive faces. They may have implications for emotion and style specifically—for example, if there is a connection between, say, emotional expression in vocalization and features of pitch contour in a particular work.

Meanwhile the use of direct evidentials contributes to the fulfillment of eliciting conditions.

4.3 The function of direct reported speech

How can the use of direct speech in people be accounted for? This question may be answered by "conservativeness" or what has been called *zerangi* of the subjects in the related literature, meaning that the speakers don't want to reveal their own intentions and they don't want to take the responsibility of others' speeches. Beeman (2016: 60) believes that if we are to investigate the relation between language and communication in Iran we should not exclude cultural considerations. He maintains that insecurity, uncertainty, and distrustfulness are the principal communicative principles in Iranian lives. He also believes that opacity in communication in their lives has its roots in what he calls *zerangi* in this culture. He defines this concept as the hiding of one's own motivation from other(s) while the other(s) know that something is happening hidden from them, but they doesn't know exactly what is taking place (ibid.: 61). Beeman rooted the concept of *zerangi* to *taghiyye* in Islam; meaning the necessity of hiding of truth when there is a bodily threat (ibid.: 56). Here we have interpreted direct speech of those who bear lack of social trust as the symptom of zerangi. It shows that they are conservative enough to use direct quotation instead of adding their own wording or interpretation to form a paraphrase for a narration. By the use of this linguistic strategy they don't take but shift the responsibility to the original (reporter) speaker. As Beeman (ibid.: 55) truly shows, the speaker who is supposedly called zerang uses some strategies to prevent his/her inner most views. As the table 4.1 shows, this effect is applied by direct speech for those who lack social trust.

Ferasatkhah (1394: 73) also believes that geographical distribution and geographical insecurity (uncertainty) directly influence the mood and behavior of the specific area. This leads to lack of principled grounds for clear dialogues and direct criticisms. "The logic of necessity" requires a distrustful environment to hide everything, including inner most intentions (ibid.: 75). This lack of clarity has been referred to in other sociologic books like that of Naraghi (2006) and Izadi (1385). So trust and self-disclosure are interconnected, and Persian speakers use reported speech to demonstrate their own trust or lack of it. Here, reported speech conceptualizes "social trust." This is called *knowledge/concept building* function of reported speech in Persian. Beeman (2016: 23) believes that the investigation into linguistic factors has been a challenge for the separation of semantics and pragmatics in Iran, for in Persian there are much more complicated relations between linguistic factors and contextual ones. This relation is in such a way that if we want to explore the nature of language and relation in Iran the social and cultural considerations must be seen and accounted for. As it is evident, Persian is a language in which syntactic structures are much simpler than stylistic variables. A Persian speaker has some linguistic choices; he can pick up and choose one of them to convey the wanted meaning based on the pragmatic considerations. Persian reported speech is also no more exception to this general principle. The semantic differences between direct and indirect speech in Persian can be summarized into some pragmatic factors like speaker/addressee personality, trust concept, and even political considerations. In other words, the meaning of Persian reported speech is determined by both textual and, more importantly, contextual factors.

Reference list

Beeman, W. (2016/1395). *Zaban, manzalat, and ghodrat in Iran. [Language, Status, and Power in Iran]*. Translated by Reza Moghaddam Kia. Tehran: Ney publication.

Ferasatkhah, M. (2015/1394). *Ma Iranian[We Iranians]*. Tehran: Ney publication.

Hogan, P. C. (2014). Stylistics, emotions, and neuroscience. In M. Burke (ed.), *The Routledge Handbook of Stylistics*. London: Routledge.

Izadi, A. M. (2006/1385). *Chera aghab mandehim? Sociology of Iranian people. [Why We Are a Backward Country]*. Tehran: Elm publication.

Naraghi, H. (2006/1385). *Jame'e shanasi Khodemani[Less Formal/ Casual Jame'e Shenasi]*. Tehran: Akhtaran publication.

5 Conclusions

5.1 Modern stylistics

In the textual interpretation technique known as stylistics, primacy is given to language. Because of the different forms, patterns, and levels that make up language, stylisticians place a high value on language. Structure is a key indicator of how well a writing will perform. Insights from, to name a few, feminist theory, cognitive theory, and discourse theory have supported established schools of current stylistics leading to feminist stylistics, cognitive stylistics, and discourse stylistics respectively. Literature, whether it be more widely read "non-canonical" kinds of writing or officially recognized "literature" as high art, is the chosen subject of study in stylistics.

Why should we practice stylistics? Exploring language, and especially the use of creativity in words, is what stylistics is all about. As a result, studying stylistics broadens our perspectives on language, and it has been noted that doing so significantly improves our comprehension of (literary) works. An analytical approach of inquiry that is intrinsically revealing emerges when we have access to the whole range of language models. Because it frequently examines texts where linguistic "rules" are bent, expanded, or otherwise altered, this style of inquiry has a significant reflective capability inasmuch as it may illuminate the same language system from which it emerges.

Here is a list of the major levels of language analysis and their related technical terms in language study, along with a brief description of what each level covers:

Level of language	Branch of language study
The *sound* of spoken language; the way words are pronounced.	phonology; phonetics
The patterns of *written* language; the shape of language on the page.	graphology

DOI: 10.4324/9781003371786-6

Level of language	Branch of language study
The way words are constructed; words and their constituent structures.	morphology
The way words combine with other words to form phrases and sentences.	syntax; grammar
The words we use; the vocabulary of a language.	lexical analysis; lexicology
The *meaning* of words and sentences.	semantics
The way words and sentences are used in everyday situations; the meaning of language in context.	pragmatics; discourse analysis

The stylistic analysis allows for the identification and elucidation of these fundamental linguistic levels. analysis itself becomes more organized and principled as a result. The natural evolution of contemporary stylistics includes a regular updating and improvement of its analytical techniques. Evidentiality is one of those new technical linguistic analyses that falls into pragmatics and discourse analysis accounts.

5.2 Literary and cognitive implications of evidentiality

The primary objective and the crucial claim of such a monograph is that evidentiality can be accounted for as a pivotal concern in stylistics and narratology. Throughout the book we have tried to show how guiding this cognitive concept is in the process of analysis of narratives. Although we have tried to depict this by the detailed analysis of data taken of Saʻdī's great literary works, namely *Būstān*, *Golestān*, and *Sonnets*,[1] here the authors are willing to provide the readers with the main arguments in favor of accounting evidentiality as a subcomponent of stylistic and narrative studies, analysis, and researches as follows:

First, we have been told that man is essentially "a story-telling animal" (Freeman 2015: 22). Narrative can be considered as a mode of understanding. From a cognitive point of view, evidentiality is a basic human cognitive mechanism by which human beings are capable of encoding source of information conveyed in their linguistic statements. Moreover, they can show their commitment, their certainty, possibility/probability, and precision in narration. Some findings from the scientific researches like that of Unal (2018) support the universalistic view of the relation between linguistic categories of evidentiality that do not shape but build on conceptual representation of source of the knowledge that are shared across the speakers of different languages. Unal reviews newly experimental evidences to assess whether the linguistic encoding of information source affects source monitoring in adults and children from different language backgrounds. In both cases, learned evidentiality in languages like Turkish is not a guide to conceptual representation of information source. It means that it is not the case that acquiring the semantics of obligatory and the frequent evidential morphemes in languages with an obligatory morpho-syntactic system of evidentiality accelerate or facilitate the development of source monitoring rather than in the case of languages without such an obligatory system. According to this research, source monitoring development occurs based on stable universal timetable and schedule. It means that cross-linguistic variation does not alter universal mechanisms of source monitoring. The same result has been proven in Mehrabi and Mahmoodi-Bakhtiari (2019b) from a processing point of view. Insofar as source monitoring is a basic human cognitive capacity, it must be considered in the analysis of narratives and styles across literary works, just as politeness principle, speech acts, and Grice cooperative principles are considered and observed. Moreover, the application of source monitoring mechanisms by a writer or poet conveys useful information about the author's mentality and sociocultural world out of which he/she has emerged. Besides, it is a common human cognitive characteristics that the generic features of the source of information matches source monitoring. If the content of a memory is highly rich in visual details, people tend to attribute it to visual perception as Johnson (2006) puts it.

Second, this topic that whether an author or poet prefers using evidentials or not (if any needed) and the use of evidential type conveys some information about the author's style and validity of the narrative at the same time. There is a body of researches that shows that direct evidentials are processed in a different manner than indirect ones. There are some cognitive findings, too, which show that direct visual/seen evidentials are much more basic cognitively and that these kinds of evidentials are processed in a different manner than the secondhand indirect evidentials like hearsay and inferences. There must be a cognitive explanation for it. Developmental researches on children show that visual access seems to be understood early. Koenig, Clement and Harris (2004) show that children report being more confident about their own knowledge when they gain it through visual access compared to being informed by someone else. Visual access is a basic perceptual mechanism in the early stages of development. In simple tasks, even three-year-olds can identify someone who has looked inside a box as knowledgeable about a box's contents over someone who has simply lifted the box (Pillow 1989; cf. Pratt and Bryant, 1990 cited in Unal, 2018). Even in Persian (Mehrabi and Mahmoodi-Bakhtiari, 2019a), the psychological reality of evidentiality hierarchy shows that direct evidentials are processed differently compared to indirect evidentials. As the data presented so far shows, Saʿdī's tendency is not to overuse evidentials in all of the literary works discussed here. What is remarkable is the overuse of direct seen evidentials in both *Golestān* and *Sonnets*. This is a crucial factor in assessing validity of his narratives discussed in Chapter 5.

Third, some kinds of evidentials help to account for the vividness of narratives that present themselves through the reader's mental imagery of the action. Through this visual mental imagery we can gain the emotional experiences of empathizing with the character(s) mentioned in narratives, so that the human cognitive system, which seems primarily designed for action, based on Ellis (2005: 25), can anticipate and foresee what will happen for us in such a situation of which narratives are telling the stories. It is through such linguistic devices that literature influences us, evidentiality being one of them. As Hagberg (2019: 1) puts it:

> There has been a vast wave of work on narrative in the last decade: this work includes numerous volumes on the philosophy of narrative and its definition, on the place of narrative in literary analysis, on the sense-making power of narrative construction, on narrative in its evolutionary aspects, and on the relation between narrative and the constitution of personhood. However, one sees less work specifically on the relations between literary narrative and self-understanding.

5.3 A snapshot of the book

This monograph tried to show how evidentiality can be accounted for as a stylistic device to show the validity of the narration, the author/poet's commitment and contribution to the narrative.

As for the detailed data of three literary works mentioned here showed, the general stylistic tendency of Saʿdī is not to use evidentials in advices and love stories, which is natural when the generic characteristics of the topic of narration is considered. But what is of the pivotal concern is Saʿdī's use of heard evidentials (in ***Būstān***) and seen evidentials (in both ***Golestān*** and ***Sonnets***) which shows the contrast between realm of "truth" as opposed to "reality."

What we as the authors of this book tried to depict is to introduce another cognitive chapter to the literary stylistics through detailed analysis of data for Saʿdī's great literary works. Such investigation is a step forward to corpus literary stylistics. This monograph introduces evidentiality to stylistic analysis of literary works. So far there has not been any research done by considering evidentiality as a stylistic strategy in general and in Persian literature, in particular; especially as a means to analyze the great works of literature, namely masterpieces, though this kind of analysis can reveal some stylistic peculiarities of great writers/poets in terms of the degree of certainty of their narratives. This investigation was only the beginning step among those attempts that may lead to a new trend in modern stylistics just as analysis of transitivity accounts for one of the linguistic variables in modern stylistics, the others being metaphor and metonymy (Simpson, 2004).

Note

1 We have considered these three as narrative texts. Narrative text is a text in which a narrative agent tells a story based on Bal (2017: 11).

Reference list

Bal, M. (2017). *Narratology: Introduction to the Theory of Narrative*. Toronto: University of Toronto Press.
Ellis, R. D. (2005). *Curious Emotions: Experiencing and the Creation of Meaning*. Amsterdam: John Benjamins.
Freeman, M. (2015). Narrative as a mode of understanding method, theory, praxis. In A. De Fina & A. Georgakopoulou (eds.), *The Handbook of Narrative Analysis*. West Sussex: Wiley Blackwell.
Hagberg, G. L. (2019). Introduction: Literary experience and self-reflection. In G. L. Hagberg (ed.), *Narrative and Self-Understanding*. New York: Palgrave.
Johnson, M. K. (2006). Memory and reality. *American Psychologist* 61: 760–771.
Koenig, M. A., F. Clement and P. L. Harris. (2004). Trust in testimony: Children's use of true and false statements. *Psychological Science* 15: 694–698.
Mehrabi, M. and B. Mahmoodi-Bakhtiari. (2019a/1398a). The psychological reality of evidentiality hierarchy in Persian during sentence listening comprehension. *Language Related Research* (in Press).
Mehrabi, M. and B. Mahmoodi-Bakhtiari. (2019b/1398b). A comparative study of evidentiality auditory comprehension of Persian, Turkish, and English. *Journal of Comparative Linguistic Researches*(in Press).
Pillow, B. (1989). Early understanding of perception as a source of knowledge. *Journal of Experimental Child Psychology* 47: 116–129.
Pratt, C. and P. Bryant. (1990). Young children understand that looking leads to knowing (so long as they are looking into a single barrel). *Child Development* 61: 973–982.
Simpson, P. (2004). *Stylistics: A Resource Book for Students*. London: Routledge.
Unal, E. (2018). Evidentials, information source, and cognition. In A. Aikhenvald (ed.), *Oxford Handbook of Evidentiality*. Oxford: Oxford University Press.

Glossary of terms

context: Either the physical context or the linguistic context (co-text) in which words are used

co-operative principle: An underlying assumption of conversation that you will "make your conversational contribution such as is required, at the stage at which it occurs, by the accepted purpose or direction of the talk exchange in which you are engaged"

corpus linguistics: The study of language in use by analyzing the occurrence and frequency of forms in a large collection of texts typically stored in a computer

corpus stylistics: The part of digital linguistics which considers the prominent style of the author based on the data revised

culture: Socially acquired knowledge

discourse analysis: The study of language beyond the sentence, in text and conversation

evidentiality: The indication of the nature of evidence for a given statement

politeness: Showing awareness and consideration of another person's public self-image

pragmatics: The study of speaker meaning and how more is communicated than is said

semantics: The study of the meaning of words, phrases, and sentences

speech act: An action such as "promising" performed by a speaker with an utterance, either as a direct speech act or an indirect speech act

speech style: A way of speaking that is either formal/careful or informal/casual

structural analysis: The investigation of the distribution of grammatical forms in a language

Index

Aikhenvald, A. 2, 6, 7, 8, 11, 13, 16, 17, 167
author 2, 3, 19, 26, 41, 48, 53, 59, 63, 66, 73, 80, 81, 83, 136, 164, 165, 168

Bal, M. 167
Barnes, J. 6, 16, 19, 26
Beeman, W. 161, 162
Bernardez, E. 23, 25, 26
Black, E. 15, 16, 18, 26
Boas, F. 1
Bor, D. 26
Boyd, B. 25, 27
Būstān vii, viii, x, 1, 2, 3, 29, 30, 41, 48, 53, 54, 59, 63, 66, 73, 76, 80, 82, 135, 136, 158, 159, 160, 164, 166

Capone, A. 19, 23, 27
Chapman, S. 18, 27
Chung, K. 5, 16
Clark, B. 18, 27
Clement, A.F. 165, 167
cognition 17, 27, 167
cognitive x, 1, 3, 4, 8, 17, 18, 20, 22, 24, 25, 27, 163, 164, 165, 166
communication 5, 6, 21, 23, 28, 161
conceptual 164, 165
context 164
contextual 23, 161, 162
Coulmus, F. 19, 20, 27

discourse x, 1, 6, 16, 18, 19, 26, 27, 28, 163, 164
discourse analysis x, 164

Edelman, G. 26
Ellis, R. D. 166, 167
evidentiality vii, viii, ix, x, xii, 1, 2, 3, 4, 5, 6, 7, 8, 9, 11, 12, 13, 14, 15, 16, 17, 18, 20, 21, 22, 24, 25, 26, 29, 82, 136, 159, 164, 165, 166, 167, 168
evidentials x, 1, 2, 4, 5, 6, 7, 8, 10, 11, 13, 14, 16, 17, 19, 21, 22, 26, 29, 30, 36, 37, 40, 41, 43, 45, 46, 48, 49, 51, 53, 54, 57, 59, 60, 61, 62, 63, 64, 65, 66, 68, 69, 70, 71, 73, 74, 75, 76, 77, 79, 80, 81, 82, 83, 84, 88, 89, 91, 92, 98, 101, 102, 104, 107, 108, 110, 111, 112, 114, 115, 116, 120, 121, 122, 123, 124, 126, 128, 129, 130, 131, 134, 135, 136, 146, 148, 157, 158, 159, 160, 165, 166, 197

Faller, M. 5, 16
Ferasatkhah, M. 161, 162
Freeman, M. 164, 167
Frith, C. 26, 27

Givön, T. 27
Goddard, C. 20, 27
Golestān vii, viii, 1, 2, 3, 83, 84, 92, 104, 111, 112, 116, 121, 124, 129, 134, 135, 136, 158, 159, 160, 164, 166
Golfam, A. 6, 13, 17, 18, 27

Habler, G. 6, 16, 18, 19, 27
Hagberg, G. L. 166, 167
Haiman, J. 19, 27
Hardy, D. E. 26, 27
Harris, P. L. 165, 167

Index

Ifantidou, E. 2, 7, 16
Izadi, A. M. 161, 162

Koenig, M. 165, 167
Krippendoff, K. 1, 29, 158
Kurzweil, R. 26, 27

Lee, J. 5, 17
Leech, G. 18
Li, C. N. 19, 20, 27

Mahlberg, M. 29, 158
Mahmoodi-Bakhtiari, B. 7, 17, 165, 167
Mason, J. 26, 27
McCready, E. 5, 17
Mehrabi, M. 7, 17, 165, 167
Morady Moghaddam, M. 4, 17, 23, 24, 26
Murray, S. 5, 17
Mushin, I. 2, 7, 17

Naraghi, H. 161, 162
narration 1, 2, 7, 15, 83, 135, 136, 161, 164, 166
narratives xi, 2, 3, 15, 17, 18, 26, 27, 83, 135, 164, 165, 166, 167
narratology x, 26, 27, 164, 167
narrator 9, 16, 83, 135

Ogata, N. 5, 17
Omidvari, A. 6, 13, 17, 18, 27

poetry x, 13
pragmatic x, 1, 2, 3, 4, 11, 16, 17, 18, 19, 23, 25, 26, 27, 162, 164
pragmatics x, 3, 18, 25, 27, 164
prose x, 3, 129, 136

quotation 1, 5, 6, 10, 21, 23, 30, 41, 48, 54, 59, 63, 66, 73, 76, 82, 83, 84, 92, 104, 111, 112, 121, 123, 124, 129, 134, 135, 158, 160, 161

Sa'dī x, 1, 2, 3, 29, 30, 41, 54, 56, 60, 63, 67, 73, 76, 83, 84, 92, 124, 129, 135, 136, 140, 147, 148, 150, 151, 152, 153, 154, 155, 156, 157, 158, 159, 164, 165, 166
seen evidential x, 1, 3, 9, 45, 53, 62, 65, 69, 79, 83, 88, 98, 107, 114, 117, 135, 136, 159, 165, 166
semantics 16, 17, 28, 161, 164, 165
Sharifian, F. 23, 26, 27, 28
Shen, D. 26, 27
Short, M. 18
Sonnets (of Sa'dī) vii, viii, x, 1, 2, 3, 36, 159, 160, 164, 166
style vii, viii, xi, 3, 12, 18, 25, 26, 135, 136, 159, 160, 163, 165
stylistics viii, x, 3, 16, 18, 25, 26, 27, 29, 162, 163, 164, 165, 167

Thompson, G. 21, 28
Thompson, S. A. 19, 27
Torabi. H. 22, 28

Unal, E. 164, 165, 167

visual evidential 1, 2, 4, 6, 7, 8, 9, 10, 11, 19, 30, 39, 41, 48, 53, 54, 59, 63, 65, 66, 73, 76, 82, 83, 84, 88, 92, 98, 104, 107, 111, 112, 114, 116, 117, 121, 122, 124, 126, 129, 130, 134, 135, 136, 146, 158, 159, 160, 165, 166

Wheeless, L. 25, 28
Wierzbicka, A. 19, 20, 25, 27, 28

Yousef, S. 22, 28

For Product Safety Concerns and Information please contact our EU representative GPSR@taylorandfrancis.com
Taylor & Francis Verlag GmbH, Kaufingerstraße 24, 80331 München, Germany

www.ingramcontent.com/pod-product-compliance
Lightning Source LLC
Chambersburg PA
CBHW051745230426
43670CB00012B/2173